NEW DIRECTIONS FOR MENTAL HEALTH SERVICES

H. Richard Lamb, *University of Southern California*
EDITOR-IN-CHIEF

Assessing and Treating Victims of Violence

John Briere
University of Southern California
School of Medicine

EDITOR

P9-DFS-110

Number 64, Winter 1994

JOSSEY-BASS PUBLISHERS
San Francisco

ASSESSING AND TREATING VICTIMS OF VIOLENCE
John Briere (ed.)
New Directions for Mental Health Services, no. 64
H. Richard Lamb, Editor-in-Chief

Microfilm copies of issues and articles are available in 16mm and 35mm,
as well as microfiche in 105mm, through University Microfilms Inc., 300
North Zeeb Road, Ann Arbor, Michigan 48106-1346.

LC 87-646993   ISSN 0193-9416   ISBN 0-7879-9991-1

NEW DIRECTIONS FOR MENTAL HEALTH SERVICES is part of The Jossey-Bass
Social and Behavioral Science Series and is published quarterly by Jossey-
Bass Inc., Publishers, 350 Sansome Street, San Francisco, California
94104-1342.

EDITORIAL CORRESPONDENCE should be sent to the Editor-in-Chief,
H. Richard Lamb, Department of Psychiatry and the Behavioral Sciences,
U.S.C. School of Medicine, 1934 Hospital Place, Los Angeles, California
90033-1071.

Cover photograph by Wernher Krutein/PHOTOVAULT © 1990.

Manufactured in the United States of America. Nearly all Jossey-Bass
books, jackets, and periodicals are printed on recycled paper that contains
at least 50 percent recycled waste, including 10 percent postconsumer
waste. Many of our materials are also printed with vegetable-based inks;
during the printing process, these inks emit fewer volatile organic com-
pounds (VOCs) than petroleum-based inks. VOCs contribute to the formation of smog.

Contents

97149

EDITOR'S NOTES

It has become an accepted fact of modern life that violence is endemic in our culture. Recent research has shown that a significant proportion of North American children are sexually, physically, or psychologically abused each year, and that the number of reports of adult rape, spousal abuse, and stranger physical assault continues to grow. Research reports are not our only source of data, however; we need only read the newspapers or watch television.

Beyond the epidemiology of societal violence per se is its impact on the mental health of those who live in our culture. Scientists and clinicians are beginning to trace the genesis of a number of psychological symptoms and disorders to childhood or adult traumatic events, many of which involve interpersonal violence. As a result, a new (thus far informal) specialty of mental health practitioners has evolved, one specifically concerned with the assessment and treatment of psychological trauma. At the same time, however, the typical front-line clinician is bound to encounter children and adults who have been victimized and who present with complex posttraumatic sequelae.

It is for both the trauma specialist and the general clinician that this volume was developed. As research and clinical practice has grappled with the issues of interpersonal violation and victimization-related syndromes, a new body of information has slowly come into focus. This material is concerned with the assessment and treatment of post-victimization trauma. The contributors to this volume are quite familiar with these issues, in several cases because of their pioneering roles as research or clinical innovators. More of the information presented here addresses sexual abuse or sexual assault than other kinds of interpersonal victimization, primarily because this area has been studied most.

The first four chapters describe the psychological sequelae of violent victimization, with a focus on critical assessment issues. In Chapter One, Diana Elliott presents an overview of assessment strategies and instruments available for the evaluation of acute victimization effects in adulthood. Chapter Two, by William Friedrich, outlines the immediate impacts of childhood sexual victimization and provides a detailed review of state-of-the-art assessment in this area. In Chapter Three, Debra Neumann presents a comprehensive review of the known longer-term effects of childhood sexual abuse and suggests a theoretical framework for organizing and understanding such sequelae. In Chapter Four, Millie Astin, Christopher Layne, Angela Camilleri, and David Foy discuss what is perhaps the most common form of violence-related psychological distress: posttraumatic stress disorder.

Chapters Five through Eight are devoted to therapeutic intervention. Cheryl Lanktree describes a model treatment program for sexually abused children and provides data-based information on effective treatment approaches with this population in Chapter Five. In Chapter Six, Barbara Gilbert describes a treatment approach for women who are victims of rape and sexual assault. In Chapter Seven, Beth Houskamp presents an overview of issues and interventions relevant to the treatment of women who have been physically assaulted by their partners. Finally, in Chapter Eight, Karin Meiselman describes her reintegration approach to the treatment of adults molested as children.

Although the subject matter of this volume is disturbing, growing assessment and treatment technology gives us hope for treating victims of violence. Nevertheless, we must be continuously aware that treatment, though extremely important, is what one does after the fact. Even more imperative is the prevention of interpersonal violence through education, early treatment of victims who otherwise might later become perpetrators, effective law enforcement, and the provision of minimal standards of health and social support for everyone in our society.

John Briere
Editor

JOHN BRIERE, Ph.D., is associate professor of psychiatry and psychology at the University of Southern California School of Medicine.

PART ONE

Assessment

Assessment of the impact of interpersonal violence can be difficult not only because of the nature of the traumatic event, but also because of the limited number of clinically useful instruments designed to assess such impact. Trauma-specific measures tend to be more helpful in this regard than generic measures of psychological distress.

Assessing Adult Victims of Interpersonal Violence

Diana M. Elliott

Research documents the high frequency of interpersonal violence in national samples of the general population. Among adult women, 13–23 percent have been raped (Kilpatrick and others, 1987; National Victim Center, 1992), approximately 11 percent have experienced aggravated assault (Kilpatrick and others, 1987; Norris, 1992), and as many as 26 percent have been battered in sexual relationships (Elliott and Briere, 1994). Although victimization rates tend to be lower for men than women, prevalence data suggest that a significant minority of males have been victimized in their lifetime. Approximately 19 percent of adult males have been the victim of aggravated assault (Norris, 1992), 2–3 percent have been raped or sexually assaulted (Elliott and Mok, 1994), and 19 percent have served in military combat (Norris, 1992). As children, 20–40 percent of women and 10–20 percent of men were sexually victimized (Finkelhor, in press), and approximately 20 percent of both men and women were physically abused (Elliott and Briere, 1994).

The trauma literature suggests that the experience of interpersonal violence is associated with increased risk for posttraumatic stress disorder (PTSD) and a wide variety of other difficulties, including affective, dissociative, somatization, and substance abuse disorders (Burnam and others, 1988; Saunders, Villeponteaux, Lipovsky, and Kilpatrick, 1992). The assessment of victims of violence is further complicated by the tendency for such individuals to present with an array of symptoms that meet diagnostic criteria in several categories (Davidson, Hughes, and Blazer, 1991). Thus, the assessment of such individuals is often complex and includes evaluations of several areas of functioning.

Of primary concern are emotional distress, cognitive distortions, physiological problems, behavioral changes, and interpersonal functioning.

Despite the wide variety of problems and diagnoses presented by victimized individuals, the experience of interpersonal violence does not necessarily mean that the individual will experience significant immediate or long-term distress. Although fewer than one out of four adults who have been exposed to a traumatic event develop posttraumatic stress disorder (Breslau, Davis, Andreski, and Peterson, 1991), as many as 57 percent of women who have been raped meet the PTSD diagnostic criteria at some point after the assault (Kilpatrick and others, 1987). Thus, knowing that an individual has been victimized is only the beginning of the clinical evaluation.

Assessment Process

The basic task of assessment is to provide a clearer picture of clinically relevant material so that an appropriate diagnosis can be made and specific treatment goals can be formulated. It may be helpful to conceptualize the assessment process as having two phases: initial and ongoing. The initial assessment phase is intended to assist in diagnosis and treatment planning, and is the focus of the current chapter. However, assessment (especially for trauma victims) should also be an ongoing process in which the clinician continually assesses the client's fluctuating posttraumatic distress, internal resources, and social functioning. Such assessment informs the clinician about where and how to intervene, based on the relative balance between client distress and client resources (Briere, in press a).

During the initial phase of treatment, however, the clinician must develop some understanding of the client's victimization experience, life history, level of distress, and social support. These data inform the clinician of the client's difficulties and vulnerabilities (such as prior psychiatric diagnoses and multiple victimization experiences) as well as the potential resources (such as intellect, motivation, and ability to self-soothe).

A formal evaluation interview typically provides extensive data that might otherwise take the clinician months to gather. As such, it is recommended whenever possible in the treatment of trauma victims. However, most people who enter treatment do so at a point of crisis, when such inquiries can be experienced as intolerable or inappropriate. Thus, the clinician must strike a balance between meeting the immediate needs of the client and obtaining the necessary information to provide appropriate intervention. The assessment process itself can be stressful for the client, who is asked not only to recount the specifics of the victimization experience, but who may for the first time realize the extent of the impact of that experience on his or her life. If formal psychological testing is to be completed, it should be separate from the therapy sessions so that the client's felt needs are addressed by the therapy.

Generic Instruments for Assessing Psychological Distress

To date, virtually all of the psychological instruments used in standard test batteries were developed without a particular focus on trauma victims. These include instruments such as the Minnesota Multiphasic Personality Inventory-2 (MMPI-2), Millon Clinical Multiaxial Inventory (MCMI-III), the Thematic Apperception Test (TAT), and the Rorschach. Recent research suggests that such instruments do not uniformly distinguish among groups of victimized versus nonvictimized individuals, or that victims of chronic trauma appear to be particularly pathological on such instruments, at least in treatment-seeking populations (Elliott, 1993a; Scott and Stone, 1986; Tsai, Feldman-Summers, and Edgar, 1979). One study (Elliott, 1993a) suggests that victimized inpatients are twice as likely to obtain invalid MMPI profiles as are their nonvictimized cohorts (30 percent versus 15 percent). It is possible that victimized individuals tend to exaggerate their distress, but it appears more likely that standard instruments fail to take into account the disorganizing impact of interpersonal violence on the client's psyche. Additionally, interpretative data for each of these measures have been developed without specific reference to victimization experiences.

Clinicians who choose to use standard instruments in the assessment of victimization should be careful in their interpretation of these data. The content of the elevated scales should be examined for their relevance to victimization issues. For example, a nineteen-year-old survivor of ten years of incest had an elevated score on the psychopathic deviant scale of the MMPI-2. Ordinarily, this would suggest hostility and aggressiveness, rebelliousness toward authority, and a high likelihood of antisocial behavior (which is how he was described by a computer-generated interpretive summary). An analysis of the item content, however, revealed high family discord and social alienation, with subclinical levels on authority problems and social imperturbability. The items endorsed were expected given his abuse history, and did not suggest antisocial traits. Thus, overreliance on such instruments (and computer-generated interpretations of the test data) can result in an overly pathological view of traumatized clients.

Trauma-Specific Measures

Although a standard test battery on a victimized individual can be helpful to the clinician who is particularly sensitive to trauma-based symptomatology, trauma-specific measures may obtain more clinically-relevant information in a less obtrusive and time-consuming manner. Some of the more common ones are discussed in terms of posttraumatic, dissociative, and other trauma-related distress.

Posttraumatic Stress. The most obvious area of distress to be assessed in trauma victims is the symptom clusters associated with posttraumatic stress disorder (PTSD) and acute stress disorder in DSM-IV (American Psychiatric Association, 1994). For a diagnosis of PTSD, the DSM-IV requires a traumatic event, subjective distress related to the trauma, and three clusters of symptoms that persist longer than one month: re-experiencing of the trauma, avoidance responses, and hyperarousal. The diagnosis of acute stress disorder appears for the first time in DSM-IV, and is an appropriate diagnosis when the distress from a trauma has persisted between two and twenty-eight days. Along with the re-experiencing, avoiding, and arousal symptoms of PTSD, acute stress disorder also includes a dissociative response to the trauma, as demonstrated by the presence of at least three of the following five symptoms: subjective numbing, reduced awareness, derealization, depersonalization, and dissociative amnesia. As of yet, there are no clinical instruments designed to assist in the diagnosis of acute stress disorder per se.

Most conventional assessment tools used in standard test batteries do not assess the three distinct clusters of symptoms related to either PTSD or acute stress disorder. Thus, although PTSD is one of the more likely diagnoses for victimized individuals, it is likely to be underdiagnosed if clinicians rely too heavily on traditional psychological test instruments.

Currently, there are several research instruments and a few clinical tests specifically intended to assess the range of posttraumatic symptomatology. The following section briefly summarizes the strengths and potential weakness of the most commonly used instruments.

Perhaps because of its utility with all forms of trauma, the Impact of Events Scale (IES) (Horowitz, Wilner, and Alvarez, 1979) is one of the most widely used assessment tools for posttraumatic symptomatology in research studies. It is a fifteen-item scale in which subjects rate the impact of a traumatic event; seven items relate to intrusive symptomatology and eight address avoidance symptoms. The reliability of this measure is good (Horowitz, Wilner, and Alvarez, 1979) and it has been shown to accurately classify true cases of DSM-III-R PTSD (Kulka and others, 1990). A primary drawback for clinicians is that the instrument is intended for research purposes, and thus no standardization data are available for clinical use. Additionally, although this instrument measures re-experiencing and avoidance symptoms, it does not assess the extent of hyperarousal experienced by the client. Additionally, it (along with all of the measures in this category) cannot be used as the sole indicator of PTSD because it does not evaluate whether the symptoms lasted longer than one month, as required by DSM-IV criteria.

Because of the paucity of useful instruments for the assessment of victimization, several authors have generated PTSD scales to assess specific types of victimization experiences. The Mississippi Scale for Combat-Related PTSD (Keane, Caddell, and Taylor, 1988) is an example. This instrument has been shown to have excellent sensitivity and specificity for combat veterans (Kulka and others, 1990). The PTSD Checklist (PCL) (Weathers and others, 1993) is a seventeen-item instrument that has also been used to assess combat-related PTSD. Unlike the Mississippi Scale, however, its items are not specifically anchored in the combat experience, and thus it has the potential for use with other forms of trauma, although such use has yet to be tested. The PTSD Symptom Scale (Foa, Riggs, Dancu, and Rothbaum, 1993) is a seventeen-item scale of posttraumatic symptomatology in sexually assaulted women. As with the PCL, its usefulness with other forms of victimization has yet to be examined. A problem with all of these scales is their lack of validity items. No data are obtained to assess the client's test-taking attitude—their willingness to over- or underendorse items—or their potential response to treatment.

Two PTSD scales have been developed on veteran samples from the MMPI-2. The MMPI-PK (Keane, Malloy, and Fairbank, 1984) is a forty-item scale that has been validated in a number of veteran samples (Keane, 1994), and the MMPI-PS scale (Schlenger and Kulka, 1989) is a sixty-item scale for which there are few data available on its utility. Neither the MMPI-PK nor the MMPI-PS should be used to make a diagnosis of PTSD, but each can provide helpful information about general emotional turmoil, with the scales including symptoms such as anxiety, sleep disturbance, guilt, depression, and disturbing thoughts.

Dissociation. Dissociation can be defined as a disruption in the normally occurring linkages between subjective awareness, feelings, thoughts, behavior, and memories, consciously or unconsciously invoked in order to reduce psychological distress (Briere, 1992). It allows victims of violent crime to separate themselves from the trauma so as to not fully realize its impact and compartmentalize their experience of the traumatic event. Many victims of chronic violence continue to experience significant levels of dissociation when the threat to physical integrity has ceased (Briere and Runtz, 1990; Chu and Dill, 1990; Lindberg and Distad, 1985). Thus, when a client presents with a history of chronic or particularly violent victimization, screening for levels of dissociation is important. Only recently, however, has this area of trauma-based distress been systematically studied.

Dissociative phenomena have never been directly evaluated by traditional psychological tests, although such tests often include dissociative items. Items suggestive of dissociation on the MMPI-2, for example, are found in the critical items and schizophrenia scale ("I often feel as if things are not real," for example). Attempts have been made to create a dissociation scale for the MMPI (such as the Perceptual Alteration Scale; see Saunders, 1986), but have met with limited success.

Alternative measures that are more directly helpful in the assessment of dissociation include the Dissociative Experiences Survey (DES) (Bernstein and Putnam, 1986) and the Structured Clinical Interview for Dissociative Disorders (SCID-D) (Steinberg, 1986). The DES is a twenty-eight-item self-report instrument that rates various aspects of dissociative experiences on a scale of

0 to 100. Normative data are available across a variety of samples and for various diagnostic categories. The Structured Clinical Interview for DSM-III-R Dissociative Disorders is a semistructured interview that evaluates five dissociative symptoms and the spectrum of dissociative disorders. Good reliability and discriminant validity have been demonstrated for the instrument (Steinberg, Rounsaville, and Cicchetti, 1990).

Multidimensional Instruments. As previously stated, interpersonal victimization can result not only in classic PTSD or dissociative symptoms, but also a wide spectrum of trauma-based distress. This appears especially relevant in more chronic victimization such as chronic childhood sexual or physical abuse, spousal rape or battery, or political imprisonment (Herman, 1992). Thus, any assessment of victimized individuals should not limit itself to screening for PTSD or dissociative disorders. Also relevant are trauma-related anger, sexual problems, cognitive distortions, somatized expression of trauma, substance abuse, interpersonal difficulties, disturbance in self functions, and tension reduction behaviors. Two assessment instruments the author has found particularly useful in screening for a wide range of post-victimization distress are the Trauma Symptom Inventory (Briere, in press *b*) and the Symptom Checklist-90R (SCL-90R) (Derogatis, 1977).

A promising new clinical instrument is the Trauma Symptom Inventory (TSI) (Briere, in press *b*), which assesses ten areas of trauma-related distress. The diagnosis of PTSD cannot be made from this psychometrically reliable 100-item instrument because the time frame of the symptoms is not anchored according to DSM-IV criteria. However, the three symptom clusters of PTSD (intrusion, avoidance, and arousal) are examined in separate scales. Also included are a variety of associated trauma-based symptom scales not typically examined in PTSD instruments, including anger, depression, dissociation, sexual difficulties, impaired self-reference, and tension reduction behavior. The clinical utility of the TSI in distinguishing various types of victimized from nonvictimized subjects has been demonstrated in clinical (Briere, Elliott, Harris, and Cotman, in press), university (Smiljanich and Briere, 1993), and general population (Elliott, 1993b) samples.

A particular advantage of the TSI is its inclusion of three validity scales, which increases its clinical utility. Additionally, the author appears to have been particularly sensitive about avoiding the inclusion of validity items that are more likely to be endorsed by traumatized individuals. Unlike the MMPI-2, for example, which contains items indicative of both PTSD (such as "I have nightmares every few nights") and dissociation (such as "My soul sometimes leaves my body") in its validity scales, the TSI validity items tapping atypical responses focus on extremely unusual or psychotic items not typically associated with normal ranges of traumatization.

Although some areas of the distress found in chronic victimization are not assessed in the TSI (such as somatizing responses, paranoid-like symptoms, cognitive distortions, and nonsexual interpersonal difficulties), the brevity of the instrument lends itself well to combination with instruments that focus on such aspects. Thus, it is recommended in any evaluation of victimization.

Symptom Checklist-90-Revised. The SCL-90R (Derogatis, 1977) is a well-established clinical test used in both research and clinical settings. This instrument provides an index of global distress as well as nine subscales assessing a variety of symptom clusters. In addition, various authors have developed PTSD scales from the SCL-90 that reliably distinguish PTSD from non-PTSD respondents and assess the impact of various traumatic experiences: crime-related PTSD (Saunders, Arata, and Kilpatrick, 1990), disaster-related PTSD (Green and others, 1994), and war-zone PTSD (Weathers and others, 1993). Additionally, these PTSD scales are highly predictive of trauma status (Saunders, Arata, and Kilpatrick, 1990).

Although this instrument provides valuable information related to psychological distress, its development without specific reference to victimization may limit its usefulness in this regard. For example, some of the items thought to be indicative of psychosis are consistent with long-term sexual abuse or battering relationships (such as feeling lonely even when you are with people and never feeling close to another person). Thus, as with other measures, item analysis is recommended when clinical elevations are reached on various scales.

Diagnostic Interviews

Several authors have recommended the use of structured interview schedules for trauma victims (Resnick, Kilpatrick, and Lipovsky, 1991; Wolfe and Keane, 1993). This recommendation is based on research that suggests that more than 50 percent of those who meet the diagnostic criteria of PTSD have coexisting Axis I diagnoses (Helzer, Robins, and McEvoy, 1987; Keane and Wolfe, 1990). Structured schedules are relatively quick to administer and provide a framework from which to evaluate a wide range of diagnostic possibilities. The format of such instruments has the advantage of providing organization while reviewing the spectrum of possible posttraumatic difficulties. Thus, the clinician obtains a broader picture of the client and gains a sense of preexisting conditions and likely coping behaviors subsequent to victimization.

The strength of the structured interview is also its drawback. Many clinicians do not like the constraints imposed on the evaluation process by such instruments. Also, such schedules do little to provide etiological information regarding the diagnoses. Nevertheless, diagnostic interviews are recommended to evaluate common forms of comorbid difficulties such as substance abuse, affective disorders, and somatizing difficulties.

The Structured Clinical Interview for the DSM-III-R (SCID) (Spitzer and Williams, 1986) is the most widely used of such instruments in PTSD studies, and has been applied across a range of trauma populations. It is highly reliable and diagnostically demonstrates good sensitivity and excellent specificity

(Kulka and others, 1990). The Diagnostic Interview Schedule (DIS) (Robins, Helzer, Croughan, and Ratliff, 1981) has been used in the study of the impacts of disaster and war trauma. However, research data have yet to establish its diagnostic usefulness with community samples. Finally, the Psychiatric Diagnostic Interview-Revised (PDI-R) (Othmer and others, 1989), although less frequently used in the study of trauma, is an easily administered instrument that screens for seventeen basic psychiatric syndromes, including PTSD, and provides both current and lifetime diagnoses. Psychometric data presented in the PDI-R manual suggest that it is both reliable and valid in terms of its diagnostic abilities across the range of diagnoses.

Trauma Interview Schedules

Although crisis intervention is likely to be helpful to victims of violence, most do not seek it out at the time of their victimization. Those who eventually seek treatment often wait an extended period of time and experience yet another crisis before entering therapy. During the time between their victimization and their presentation to a clinician, it is likely that such clients have made certain idiosyncratic adaptations to the impact of the trauma. Additionally, people who experience one traumatic event are often revictimized (Kilpatrick and others, 1987; Kulka and others, 1990). Given the time lapse that often occurs between victimization and treatment, as well as the possibility of multiple victimization experiences, it is wise to routinely evaluate for a wide variety of life stressors in adults who presents for a clinical assessment or intervention. Three useful instruments in this regard are the Potential Stressor Experiences Inventory (Kilpatrick and others, 1987), the Traumatic Stress Schedule (TSS) (Norris, 1990), and the Traumatic Events Scale (TES) (Elliott, 1992).

The Potential Stressor Experiences Inventory (Kilpatrick and others, 1987) is a well-designed structured interview administered by a clinician or trained layperson. It is used to assess various forms of interpersonal violence as well as a range of other potentially stressful events (such as financial stress and family illness). Depending on the number of traumatic events, the interview takes between twenty-five and ninety minutes. As of yet, no reliability or validity data are available on this instrument.

The Traumatic Stress Schedule (TSS) (Norris, 1990) is an alternative structured screening instrument that can be administered by a trained layperson and completed relatively quickly. The uniqueness of this instrument is that it combines the screen for trauma with a brief assessment of trauma-related distress, primarily in terms of intrusive and avoidance symptoms. As with all instruments of this kind, the reliability and validity have yet to be established. A disadvantage of the schedule is its lack of behavioral definitions in certain categories. For example, childhood and adult sexual assault is screened by asking "Did anyone ever make you have sex by using force or threatening to harm you? This includes any type of unwanted sexual activity" (Norris, 1992, p. 411).

The Traumatic Events Scale (TES) (Elliott, 1992) is a self-administered instrument that assesses the incidence and frequency of twenty forms of interpersonal violence, traumatic grief, and natural disasters. Also assessed is the client's subjective response to the trauma. The self-administration of the instrument is an advantage of the TES, requiring clinical follow-up only on endorsed items. However, as with the other schedules, no test–retest reliability or validity data are available on this instrument.

Other Issues in Assessment

Authors such as Herman (1992) have suggested that victims of chronic violence often present with a complex array of symptoms that do not conform easily to diagnostic criteria. Many victims present with symptoms seen in various personality disorders (Briere, 1992). Such symptoms could obviously be indicative of an actual preexisting personality dysfunction in the victim. Alternatively, clients who present with symptoms of personality disorders may be expressing transient distress reflective of victimization dynamics. Isolating the victim, for example, is a common practice among batterers and hostage-takers. Such a practice is apt to increase, at least temporarily, the victim's dependent or passive traits. An individual who, following a kidnapping and rape, presents with strong paranoid-like features may be displaying transient idiosyncratic responses to recent life events, a stress-related exacerbation of pretrauma Axis I difficulties, or ongoing personality disturbance seen throughout the client's adult life. The basic issue in the Axis II diagnoses, however, is the chronicity of symptoms across time and setting. The clinician is apt to become clearer regarding these issues only through diligent attention to pre- and posttrauma functioning throughout the treatment process, rather than being able to make definitive conclusions in the initial assessment process.

A careful lifetime history of the individual's adjustment before and after traumatic events is necessary in order that both the client and therapist make reasonable treatment goals and evaluate the likely course of treatment. Research data suggest that certain factors increase the victim's risk of developing more than transitory distress. Individuals at greater risk for developing posttraumatic difficulties include those with genetic vulnerability to psychiatric disturbance (Breslau, Davis, Andreski, and Peterson, 1991; Kulka and others, 1990), early exposure to traumatic events (Davidson, Hughes, and Blazer, 1991), previctimization psychiatric difficulties (Breslau, Davis, Andreski, and Peterson, 1991; McFarlane, 1989), recent life stressors or posttrauma life changes (McFarlane, 1989), lack of social support (Ruch and Chandler, 1983), substance abuse (Breslau, Davis, Andreski, and Peterson, 1991), and perceived locus of control (Kushner, Riggs, Foa, and Miller, 1993). Thus, each of these factors should be evaluated when taking the client's life history in the initial evaluation.

Summary

The assessment of the impacts of interpersonal violence on the client is an important therapeutic process that is likely to improve the quality of care provided by the clinician. Such assessment must, however, be based on an understanding of the logical consequences of violence on the victim's psyche. Additionally, the evaluator must be aware of the theoretical orientation, item content, intended use, and normative data available for the instruments used in any evaluation process. Based on available clinical and research data, trauma-specific measures are likely to be more helpful in providing relevant clinical information on the psychological status of victims of violence than are more generic measures of psychological distress.

References

American Psychiatric Association. *Diagnostic and Statistical Manual of Mental Disorders.* (4th ed.) Washington, D.C.: American Psychiatric Association, 1994.

Bernstein, E. M., and Putnam, F. "Development, Reliability, and Validity of a Dissociation Scale." *Journal of Nervous and Mental Disorders,* 1986, *174,* 727–735.

Breslau, N., Davis, G. C., Andreski, P., and Peterson, E. "Traumatic Events and Posttraumatic Stress Disorder in an Urban Population of Young Adults." *Archives of General Psychiatry,* 1991, *48,* 216–222.

Briere, J. *Child Abuse Trauma: Theory and Treatment of the Lasting Effects.* Newbury Park, Calif.: Sage, 1992.

Briere, J. "Addressing Trauma and Self Issues in Therapy for Adults Abused as Children." In J. Briere and others (eds.), *The APSAC Handbook of Child Maltreatment.* Newbury Park, Calif.: Sage, in press *a.*

Briere, J. *Professional Manual for the Trauma Symptom Inventory.* Odessa, Fla.: Psychological Assessment Resources, in press *b.*

Briere, J., Elliott, D. M., Harris, K., and Cotman, A. "Trauma Symptom Inventory: Psychometrics and Association with Childhood and Adult Victimization in Clinical Samples." *Journal of Interpersonal Violence,* in press.

Briere, J., and Runtz, M. "Differential Adult Symptomatology Associated with Three Types of Child Abuse Histories." *Child Abuse and Neglect,* 1990, *14,* 357–364.

Burnam, M. A., Stein, J. A., Golding, J. M., Siegel, J., Sorenson, S. B., Forsythe, A. B., and Telles, C. A. "Sexual Assault and Mental Disorders in Community Population." *Journal of Consulting and Clinical Psychology,* 1988, *56,* 843–851.

Chu, J. A., and Dill, D. L. "Dissociative Symptoms in Relation to Childhood Physical and Sexual Abuse." *American Journal of Psychiatry,* 1990, *147,* 887–892.

Davidson, J.R.T., Hughes, D. L., and Blazer, D. G. "Posttraumatic Stress Disorder in the Community: An Epidemiological Study." *Psychological Medicine,* 1991, *21,* 713–721.

Derogatis, L. R. *The SCL-90 Manual: Scoring, Administration and Procedures for the SCL-90.* Baltimore: Clinical Psychometrics Unit, John Hopkins University School of Medicine, 1977.

Elliott, D. M. *Traumatic Events Survey.* Unpublished psychological test. Los Angeles: Harbor-UCLA Medical Center, 1992.

Elliott, D. M. *Assessing the Psychological Impact of Recent Violence in an Inpatient Setting.* Paper presented at the annual meeting of the International Society for Traumatic Stress Studies, San Antonio, Tex., 1993a.

Elliott, D. M. *The Impact of Child Versus Adult Trauma in the General Population: Gender and Age Differences.* Paper presented at the annual meeting of the International Society for Traumatic Stress Studies, San Antonio, Tex., 1993b.

Elliott, D. M., and Briere, J. *Trauma and Dissociated Memory: Prevalence Across Events.* Paper presented at the annual meeting of the International Society for Traumatic Stress Studies, Chicago, Aug. 1994.

Elliott, D. M., and Mok, D. "Adult Sexual Assault: Prevalence, Symptomatology, and Sex Differences in the General Population." Unpublished manuscript, 1994.

Finkelhor, D. "Current Information on the Scope and Nature of Child Sexual Abuse." *The Future of Children,* 1994, *4,* 31–53.

Foa, E. B., Riggs, D. S., Dancu, C. V., and Rothbaum, B. O. "Reliability and Validity of a Brief Instrument Assessing Post-Traumatic Stress Disorder." *Journal of Traumatic Stress,* 1993, *6,* 459–474.

Green, B. L., and others. "Children and Disaster: Age, Gender, and Parental Effects on PTSD Symptoms." *Journal of the American Academy of Child and Adolescent Psychiatry,* 1994, *30,* 945–951.

Helzer, J. E., Robins, L. N., and McEnvoy, L. "Post-Traumatic Stress Disorder in the General Population: Findings of the Epidemiological Catchment Area Study." *New England Journal of Medicine,* 1987, *137,* 1630–1634.

Herman, J. L. *Trauma and Recovery: The Aftermath of Violence.* New York: Basic Books, 1992.

Horowitz, M., Wilner, N., and Alvarez, W. "Impact of Events Scale: A Measure of Subjective Stress." *Psychosomatic Medicine,* 1979, *41,* 209–218.

Keane, T. M., Caddell, J. M., and Taylor, K. L. "Mississippi Scale for Combat-Related Posttraumatic Stress Disorder: Three Studies in Reliability and Validity." *Journal of Consulting and Clinical Psychology,* 1988, *56,* 85–90.

Keane, T. M., Malloy, P. F., and Fairbank, J. A. "Empirical Development of an MMPI Subscale for the Assessment of Combat-Related Posttraumatic Stress Disorder." *Journal of Consulting and Clinical Psychology,* 1984, *52,* 888–891.

Keane, T. M., and Wolfe, J. "Comorbidity in Post-Traumatic Stress Disorder: An Analysis of Community and Clinical Studies." *Journal of Applied Social Psychology,* 1990, *20,* 1776–1788.

Kilpatrick, D. G., Saunders, B. E., Veronen, L. J., Best, C. L., and Von, J. M. "Criminal Victimization: Lifetime Prevalence, Reporting to Police, and Psychological Impact." *Crime and Delinquency,* 1987, *33,* 479–489.

Kulka, R. A., Schlenger, W. E., Fairbank, J. A., Jordan, B. K., Hough, R. L., Marmar, C. R., and Weiss, D. S. *Trauma and the Vietnam War Generation: Report of Findings from the National Vietnam Veterans Readjustment Study.* New York: Brunner/Mazel, 1990.

Kushner, M. G., Riggs, D. S., Foa, E. S., and Miller, S. M. "Perceived Controllability and Development of Posttraumatic Stress Disorder (PTSD) in Crime Victims." *Behavior Research and Therapy,* 1993, *31,* 105–110.

Lindberg, F. H., and Distad, L. J. "Post-Traumatic Stress Disorders in Women Who Experienced Childhood Incest." *Child Abuse and Neglect,* 1985, *9,* 329–334.

McFarlane, A. C. "The Aetiology of Posttraumatic Stress Morbidity: Predisposing, Precipitating and Perpetuating Factors." *British Journal of Psychiatry,* 1989, *154,* 221–228.

National Victim Center and Crime Victims Research and Treatment Center. *Rape in America: A Report to the Nation.* Washington, D.C.: National Victim Center and Crime Victims Research, 1992.

Norris, F. H. "Epidemiology of Trauma: Frequency and Impact of Different Potentially Traumatic Events on Different Demographic Groups." *Journal of Consulting and Clinical Psychology,* 1992, *60,* 409–418.

Othmer, E., Penick, E., Powell, B., Read, M., and Othmer, S. C. *Psychiatric Diagnostic Interview—Revised.* Los Angeles: Western Psychological Services, 1989.

Resnick, H. S., Kilpatrick, D. G., and Lipovsky, J. A. "Assessment of Rape-Related Post-traumatic Stress Disorder: Stressor and Symptom Dimensions." *Psychological Assessment,* 1991, *3,* 561–572.

Robins, L. N., Helzer, J. E., Croughan, J. L., and Ratliff, K. S. "NIMH Diagnostic Interview Schedule: Its History, Characteristics, and Validity." *Archives of General Psychiatry,* 1981, *38,* 381–389.

Ruch, L. O., and Chandler, S. M. "Sexual Assault Trauma During the Acute Phase: An Exploratory Model and Multivariate Analysis." *Journal of Health and Social Behavior,* 1983, *24,* 184–185.

Saunders, B. E., Arata, C. M., and Kilpatrick, D. G. "Development of a Crime-Related Post-Traumatic Stress Disorder Scale for Women Within the Symptom Checklist-90-Revised." *Journal of Traumatic Stress,* 1990, *3,* 267–277.

Saunders, B. E., Villeponteaux, L. A., Lipovsky, J. A., and Kilpatrick, D. G. "Child Sexual Assault as a Risk Factor for Mental Disorder Among Women: A Community Survey." *Journal of Interpersonal Violence,* 1992, *7,* 189–204.

Saunders, S. "The Perceptual Alteration Scale: A Scale Measuring Dissociation." *American Journal of Clinical Hypnosis,* 1986, *29,* 95–102.

Schlenger, W. E., and Kulka, R. A. *PTSD Scale Development for the MMPI-2.* Research Triangle Park, N.C.: Research Triangle Institute, 1989.

Scott, R. L., and Stone, D. A. "MMPI Profile Constellations in Incest Families." *Journal of Consulting and Clinical Psychology,* 1986, *54,* 364–368.

Smiljanich, K., and Briere, J. *Sexual Abuse History and Trauma Symptoms in a University Sample.* Paper presented at the annual meeting of the American Psychological Association, Toronto, Canada, Aug. 1993.

Spitzer, R. L., and Williams, J. B. *Structured Clinical Interviews for the DSM-III: Non-Patient Version (SCID-NP-86).* New York: Biometrics Research Department, New York State Psychiatric Institute, 1986.

Steinberg, M. *The Structured Clinical Interview for DSM-III-R Dissociative Disorders.* New Haven, Conn.: Department of Psychiatry, Yale University School of Medicine, 1986.

Steinberg, M., Rounsaville, B., and Cicchetti, D. "The Structured Clinical Interview for DSM-III-R Dissociative Disorders: Preliminary Report on a New Diagnostic Instrument." *American Journal of Psychiatry,* 1990, *147,* 76–81.

Tsai, M., Feldman-Summers, S., and Edgar, M. "Childhood Molestation: Variables Related to Differential Impacts on Psychosexual Functioning in Adult Women." *Journal of Abnormal Psychology,* 1979, *88,* 407–417.

Weathers, F. W., Litz, B. T., Keane, T. M., Herman, D. S., Steinberg, H. R., Huska, J. A., and Kraemer, H. C. *The Utility of the SCL-90-R for the Diagnosis of War-Zone Related Post-Traumatic Stress Disorder.* Unpublished manuscript, 1993.

Wolfe, J., and Keane, T. M. "New Perspectives in the Assessment and Diagnosis of Combat-Related Post-Traumatic Stress Disorder." In J. Wilson and B. Raphael (eds.), *International Handbook of Traumatic Stress Syndrome.* New York: Plenum, 1993.

DIANA M. ELLIOTT, Ph.D., *is director of training and research at the Harbor-UCLA Child Abuse Crisis Center and assistant clinical professor of psychiatry at UCLA School of Medicine.*

A framework for the psychological evaluation of child sexual abuse victims is presented, with an emphasis on abuse-specific measures that evaluate the domains of attachment, dysregulation, and issues of self.

Assessing Children for the Effects of Sexual Victimization

William N. Friedrich

Evaluating the effects of sexual abuse presents a different task to the clinician than evaluating children with specific diagnoses such as depression, anxiety, or attentional problems. There are several reasons for this difference, the first being that sexual abuse is a heterogenous phenomenon that varies from child to child in terms of the nature and severity of the abuse. Second, a broad range of children of differing developmental levels are victimized and this combination has numerous permutations, each reflected in a variety of possible symptom manifestations. Third, for evaluations to be valid, it is critical to obtain information from both parents and children about the child's functioning. However, it may be very difficult for parents to be objective about their child's functioning, especially if there are legal threats to the family's unity.

As if these were not enough complications, a further obstacle is that to date, assessment research with sexually abused children has not been driven by a clear theoretical framework (Kendall-Tackett, Williams, and Finkelhor, 1993). Rather, most of the available research has reflected typical clinical practice and has not been based on coping or trauma-impact theories.

Because of the complexity of sexual abuse effects, a combination of theories is most appropriate to direct assessment. The impact of abuse is reflected by disturbances in at least three areas of functioning: attachment, dysregulation, and issues of self (Friedrich, in press). Attachment-related variables include the quality of the parent-child relationship, whether the parents are supportive of the child, and the relative isolation of the child and family from supportive networks. Dysregulation-related variables include stress, family chaos, parental conflict, PTSD symptoms, and socioeconomic capabilities. Self issues can include the victimization history of the parent as well as the parent and child's resilience and problem-solving capabilities.

This tripartite model is supported by Briere and Runtz, (1993), who suggest that the long-term sequelae of sexual abuse are reflected in six areas: posttraumatic stress, cognitive distortions, altered emotionality, disturbed relatedness, avoidance, and impaired self-reference. These six areas are readily subsumed within the domains of attachment, dysregulation, and self. For example, attachment includes disturbed relatedness as well as avoidance. Dysregulation is reflected in posttraumatic stress and altered emotionality. Issues of self pertain to both cognitive distortions and impaired self-reference.

Traditional Versus Specialty Measures

Initial studies on the psychological evaluation of sexually abused children routinely found difficulties with generic measures of such concepts as depression and self-esteem. For example, self-esteem was the symptom with the lowest percentage of studies in which a difference was found between sexually abused and nonabused children (Kendall-Tackett, Williams, and Finkelhor, 1993). Low self-esteem is common in many children and has numerous causes. It is likely that this contributed to the relatively few between-group differences.

The behavioral assessment of sexually abused children has found that a large percentage, more than 30 percent, will show no significant behavior problems on broad-based child behavior rating scales (Kendall-Tackett, Williams, and Finkelhor, 1993). The large number of asymptomatic children may simply reflect the variability of response to sexual abuse, with children who had less severe abuse presumably showing fewer problems. However, behavior ratings completed by parents measure only overt behavior, and may not be sensitive to more subtle or hidden problems. In addition, behavior ratings can reflect parental biases to either overreport or underreport symptoms.

A study quite relevant to this issue was completed by Everson and colleagues (1989). They found that whether mothers supported their child's disclosure was directly related to the validity of their report of their child's behavior problems. Children who were supported by their mothers were evaluated in a manner that was consistent with how the evaluating psychologist saw them. That was not true for children whose mothers did not support their disclosure.

The considerable variability in preadolescent sexual abuse victims is borne out in a cluster analytic study completed on 384 children (Friedrich, 1994a). All of these children had documented sexual abuse, and each child had been rated by his or her primary female caregiver on at least the Child Behavior Checklist (Achenbach and Edelbrock, 1983). At least eight clusters emerged, including asymptomatic (37 percent), anxious or agitated (15.9 percent), sexualized (8.6 percent), aggressive (8.1 percent), depressed or withdrawn (7.6 percent), aggressive and sexualized (6 percent), anxious-sexualized (4.9 percent), and a group that was not clustered but exhibited diverse symptomatology (12 percent).

Briere (1992) noted the need for sexual abuse-specific measures to take the place of generic measures of outcome. One example is the Trauma Symptom Checklist for Children (TSCC) (Briere, in press *a*), whose scales assess generic domains of anxiety, depression, and anger, as well as three abuse-specific domains: posttraumatic stress, sexual concerns, and dissociation.

Other child-relevant sexual abuse-specific measures include the Child Sexual Behavior Inventory (Friedrich and others, 1992), the Child Dissociative Checklist (Putnam, Helmers, and Trickett, 1993), the Children's Impact of Traumatic Events Scale (Wolfe, Wolfe, and LaRose, 1986), and the Sexual Abuse Fear Evaluation (Wolfe and Wolfe, 1986). The Child Sexual Behavior Inventory (CSBI) is a thirty-six-item measure of sexual behavior in two- to twelve-year-old children. Both the original as well as the revised version reliably discriminate sexually abused from nonabused children (Friedrich, 1993). The latest version of the CSBI contains several lie items and is being normed on three groups: nonabused, nonpsychiatric children; nonabused psychiatric children; and sexually abused children. Using a nonabused psychiatric sample is important because there is evidence that nonabused children with psychiatric problems also exhibit sexual behavior problems, although not to the extent of sexually abused children and adolescents (Friedrich, Jaworski, Huxsahl, and Bengston, 1994).

The Child Dissociative Checklist (Putnam, Helmers, and Trickett, 1993) is a twenty-item measure that has demonstrated empirical validity in discriminating children who have a dissociative disorder from multiple personality disorder from normals. Dissociation is a commonly identified sequela of sexual abuse, but empirical evaluation of this phenomenon in sexually abused children is markedly lacking (Kendall-Tackett, Williams, and Finkelhor, 1993).

The revised version of the Children's Impact of Traumatic Events Scale-Revised (CITES-R) is a seventy-eight-item measure that assesses four broad categories of abuse-specific sequelae. These include PTSD, attributions about the abuse, eroticism, and social reactions (Wolfe and others, 1992). Vicki Wolfe and colleagues have also developed the Sexual Abuse Fear Evaluation (SAFE), which is a modified fear schedule assessing both general fears as well as more abuse-specific fears (Wolfe and Wolfe, 1986).

Disclosing Versus Nondisclosing Children

Because disclosure is usually disruptive to family functioning, the child's openness is related to the validity of test results. Elliott and Briere (1994) evaluated 363 children and adolescents who had been referred for psychological evaluation because of suspicions of sexual abuse. Referrals were grouped into four categories based on disclosure and medical evidence. Children who disclosed abuse in the interview scored higher on the various scales of the Trauma Symptom Checklist for Children (TSCC) (Briere, in press *a*). Children who presented with medical evidence or other strong reason to believe that they were sexually abused but who did not disclose scored significantly lower on TSCC scales than did other children, including those who had not been sexually abused. This finding strongly suggests that children's responses to assessment measures are directly related to their level of abuse disclosure or parental permission to disclose.

The Elliott and Briere (1994) study provides a context from which to view disclosure-related research, such as that of Lamb, Sternberg, and Esplin (in press). The latter authors evaluated factors that influenced the reliability and validity of statements made by young victims of sexual maltreatment. They describe a technique, criterion-based content analysis (CBCA), used to rate statements of sexually abused children. CBCA uses five broad criteria to rate children's statements. These include the coherence and informativeness of the statement, specific contents, peculiarities of content, and motivation-related criteria. Motivation-related criteria reflect a belief that a subset of children attempt to "sell" their story to the evaluator.

As we have seen above, children who are sexually abused may or may not disclose. Criticism of CBCA is identical to other criticism of using a single, generic approach to assess sexually abused children. Sexual abuse is an extremely diverse and variable phenomenon, and the ability of children to report information, either about the abuse or their subsequent feelings, varies widely. In addition, there is no single technique that reliably identifies sexually abused children (Kendall-Tackett, Williams, and Finkelhor, 1993).

Theoretically Based Assessment

The information summarized above indicates that abuse-specific approaches that assess children who are able to disclose their abuse are likely to be the most valid. Parent and child input on the dimensions of attachment, dysregulation, and self-perception of the abused child can create a contextually and developmentally sensitive assessment.

Attachment. Alexander (1992) has discussed three features that pertain to the attachment of sexually abused children to their significant caregivers. These include rejection, role reversal, and unresolved loss in the life history of the caregiver. How might attachment, or the quality of relationships in general, be assessed in the sexually abused child, both for empirical purposes and for recommending treatment?

Parents. The capacity of parents to securely attach to their child is critical to understanding the child. Several domains are pertinent. These include overt rejection or ambivalence regarding the child, other examples of a disturbed relationship, including enmeshment and role reversal, as well as unresolved loss. Disorganized attachment in infants was related to unresolved loss in parents (Main and Hesse, 1990). Mothers with a history of sexual abuse were also found to use their child for emotional support more than mothers without an abuse history (Burkett, 1991). Mothers with a sexual abuse history may be less available to meet the emotional needs of their sexually abused child. However, the direct observation of parents and children is an assessment strategy difficult to carry out in a clinical setting, and few pencil-and-paper measures are pertinent, particularly with parents of sexually abused children.

The Family Environment Scale (FES) (Moos, 1974) can be completed by both parents and children. Salient domains for sexually abused children include family cohesion, expressiveness, and conflict. Incest family dynamics suggest enmeshment, but victim-perpetrator enmeshment was not found in one FES related study (Hanson, Saunders, and Lipovsky, 1992), although more relationship problems were reported between child victims and their father perpetrator than with their mother (Lipovsky, Saunders, and Hanson, 1992). There are a variety of incestuous family types and current measures may not be sensitive to sexual-abuse-specific issues.

The negative projection subscale from the Parentification of Children Scale (Friedrich and Reams, 1993) measures parental rejection and scapegoating. In a sample of young children with a history of incestuous sexual abuse, the parental support of the child, including removing the perpetrator from the home, was inversely and significantly related to negative projection. Negative projection scores were also significantly higher for mothers with a personal history of sexual abuse than for mothers without a history of sexual abuse (Friedrich, 1994b).

Related to parental attachment are items from the Untreatable Families Checklist (Friedrich, 1990). This is a ten-item scale completed by the evaluating clinician. It rates such dimensions as maternal involvement in the victimization, rejection of the child in one form or the other, and more long-lasting abuse suggestive of parental neglect. The mean score for families where parental rights were terminated following sexual abuse was very high, as was the mean score for families where children remained for more than two years in foster care (Friedrich, 1994b).

Children. Because the child's experience of support by the parent seems to moderate the impact of sexual abuse (Friedrich, 1988), it would be useful to assess the child's sense of connection to the parent. The clinician must assess whether the child feels supported by the nonoffending parent, whether the child experiences blame or rejection because of the abuse, and whether he or she views the nonoffending parent as a secure base.

A range of generic measures could assess the quality of the child's relationship to the offending or nonoffending parent. Several of these are quasiprojective in nature and include the Kinetic Family Drawing (Burns and Kaufman, 1972), several Rorschach variables including human content and cooperation (Exner, 1974), Attachment Stories (Bretherton, Ridgeway, and Cassidy, 1990), and the Family Relations Test (Bene and Anthony, 1976). However, there is very little research examining attachment in sexually abused children.

Dysregulation. Family-based features pertinent to dysregulation include chaos, aggression, and physical abuse or battering. Alcoholic families also add to the child's feeling out of control. Other features pertinent to dysregulation in the sexually abused child include panic, dissociation, posttraumatic stress disorder, and, in a related vein, attentional difficulties caused by preoccupation or PTSD-related symptoms.

Parents. Parents with unresolved abuse issues have difficulty providing the secure base needed for children who feel out of control. The Trauma Symptom Inventory (Briere, in press *b*) is very appropriate for use with parents who have a victimization history. In addition, screening for chemical dependency is strongly recommended.

It is very useful to separately assess stressful life events in the family, such as family violence. Life stress was shown to be significantly related to the clinical presentation of sexually abused children (Friedrich and others, 1992). Domestic violence was related to child distress (Sternberg, Lamb, Greenbaum, and Cicchetti, 1993), and family risk or disruption was related to dissociation (Malinosky-Rummell and Hoier, 1991).

Children. Objective and projective measures exist to directly assess children along a range of symptoms germane to dysregulation. Sexually reactive behavior is reflective of dysregulation, and can include precocious sexual knowledge, excessive sexual behavior, sexual anxiety, eroticizing relationships, and sexual meaning. Other symptom clusters include PTSD and dissociation.

Child-related measures include the PTSD items from the Child Behavior Checklist (Wolfe and Gentile, 1993), the Child Dissociative Checklist (Putnam, Helmers, and Trickett, 1993), and the Child Sexual Behavior Inventory (Friedrich and others, 1992). All of these are completed by the parent. Wolfe has separately analyzed twenty items from the Child Behavior Checklist (Achenbach and Edelbrock, 1983) to form a PTSD scale. Sexually abused girls scored significantly higher on these items than nonabused children drawn from the Child Behavior Checklist normative sample (Wolfe and Gentile, 1993). Friedrich and Share (1994) examined children's responses to a sexual content card from the Roberts Apperception Test for Children (McArthur and Roberts, 1982). Sexually abused children report more sexual content than a psychiatric comparison group. Sexually abused children also are more likely to have sexual content in their Rorschach protocols (Friedrich, Einbender, and McCarthy, 1994). In addition, six of ten of the sexual concerns items of the Trauma Symptom Checklist for Children differ between sexually abused and psychiatric-nonabused children and adolescents (Friedrich, Jaworski, Huxsahl, and Bengston, 1994).

Instruments to assess dissociation in children are only now being developed. However, a recent study found sexually abused girls to differ from nonabused girls on three measures of dissociation, including parent report and self-report (Malinosky-Rummell and Hoier, 1991). The majority of items from the dissociation scale of the TSCC (Briere, in press *a*) discriminate sexually abused from nonabused children, even when psychiatric controls were used as a third comparison group (Friedrich, Jaworski, Huxsahl, and Bengston, 1994).

The assessment of PTSD symptoms is still evolving. PTSD-specific structural interviews found almost half of ninety-two sexual abuse victims to meet DSM-IIIR criteria for PTSD (McLeer, Deblinger, Henry, and Orvaschel, 1992). In addition, a number of children exhibited partial PTSD symptoms. An almost identical frequency was found in a study using a PTSD-sensitive diagnostic interview (Adam, Everett, and O'Neal, 1992).

The Rorschach-related PTSD index developed by Judith Armstrong (1991) discriminates sexually abused from nonabused girls (Friedrich, Einbender, and McCarthy, 1994). This index includes the sum of anatomy, blood, sex, morbid, and aggressive content.

Self-medication of sexual abuse-related symptoms implies attempts at self-regulation. Two studies found more substance abuse in sexually abused adolescent inpatients than in their nonabused counterparts (Hussey and Singer, 1993; Hussey, Strom, and Singer, 1992). However, chemical abuse in sexually abused adolescents can reflect both parental modeling and the adolescent's efforts at self-medication (Hernandez, 1992).

Self-Representation. The self is an ever-evolving entity that is central to a sense of identity, a capacity for resilience, potency, and an ongoing stable frame of reference. Included in sexual-abuse-specific self issues are experiences of fragmentation, shame, reduced self-efficacy, and body integrity.

Parents. Personality stability in the parents fosters the emergence of a sense of self and promotes the child's ability to accurately report his or her feelings and to develop an integrated self-representation. Understanding the child without an awareness of the parents' general personality problems is extremely difficult. For example, Friedrich (1991) used the MMPI and found that mothers of sexually abused children differed from mothers presenting for outpatient therapy. Parents of sexually abused children were likely to be significantly more angry and inconsistent with their child. This was particularly true for parents with a sexual abuse history. In fact, the severity of the parents' problems was related to the length of the child's victimization. Combining the MMPI with the Trauma Symptom Inventory (Briere, in press *b*) can provide additional, abuse-specific information.

Children. The assessment of self in the sexually abused child must focus on areas more germane to the sexual abuse experience, including body perception and sexual meaning. In an ongoing study, we are examining these variables (Marquardt and Friedrich, 1994). Sexual meaning scores are significantly different between sexually abused adolescents and their nonabused psychiatric counterparts. Our findings echo other research with sexually abused male adolescents, who reported more concerns about their appearance than their nonabused counterparts (Hussey, Strom, and Singer, 1992).

The abuse attribution factor of the CITES-R (Wolfe and others, 1991) includes the following trauma-specific subscales: self-blame and guilt, vulnerability, empowerment, and dangerous world. These dimensions overlap with the four subscales from the Children's Attributions and Perceptions Scale (CAPS) (Mannarino, Cohen, and Berman, 1994): feeling different from peers, interpersonal trust, self-blame, and perceived credibility. The authors recently reported that the first three of the four CAPS subscales significantly differed between sexually abused and nonabused controls.

Somatic complaints are another manifestation of self-representation. Body integrity is a reflection of one's sense of self. Sexually abused children exhibit significantly more somatic complaints (Friedrich and Schafer, in press), particularly for such symptoms as nausea and stomach aches.

Projective assessment of the self would include Human Figure Drawings, Sentence Completion, and the Rorschach. Results are mixed for Human Figure Drawings with sexually abused children (Chantler, Pelco, and Mertin, 1993). However, on the Sentence Completion Test (Loevinger and Wessler, 1970), sexually abused girls report more often than nonabused girls that "the worst thing about being a woman is having your period" (Friedrich, 1994b). This also reflects discomfort with sexually related physical aspects of self.

Summary

In summary, the psychological assessment of sexually abused children is complicated significantly by the fact that there is no single syndrome that reflects the impact of sexual abuse (Kendall-Tackett, Williams, and Finkelhor, 1993). A number of generic measures of psychopathology in children continue to find large percentages of children relatively asymptomatic. This is due to the variability in impact of sexual abuse, but also reflects the need to develop abuse-specific outcome measures.

Because we are discussing the evaluation of children, psychological assessment must be developmentally sensitive and reflect the context of the child (Stewart, Bussey, Goodman, and Saywitz, 1993). Consequently, information should be obtained not only from parents and children, but from the entire family. Unless an evaluation includes some abuse-specific measures and examines findings about the child in the context of the larger family environment, it is not likely to be valid.

The interrelationship of abuse impact on parental perception and subsequent parental accuracy in reporting also must be examined in more detail. Not surprisingly, maternal reports of their sexually abused child's emotional states are strongly correlated with their own distress (Newberger, Geremy, Waternaux, and Newberger, 1993). This confound necessitates input from teachers or other objective observers of the child.

The evaluation of sexually abused children should be theoretically driven. I strongly recommend assessing both the child and the parents with regard to attachment quality, difficulties with self-regulation, and an impaired sense of self. There are a number of measures pertinent to both parents and children across each of these domains. However, measures must be developed and validated that allow for parent, child, and teacher report in the areas of sexual behavior, sexual concerns, sexual meaning, body integrity, abuse-specific aspects of self (such as blame, shame, and dissociation), PTSD, abuse-specific fears, and family-related variables of rejection and role reversal. There is a developing literature that supports the need to assess each of these domains in a multimodal manner.

References

Achenbach, T. M., and Edelbrock, C. *Manual for the Child Behavior Checklist and Revised Child Behavior Profile.* Burlington: Department of Psychiatry, University of Vermont, 1983.

Adam, B. S., Everett, B. L., and O'Neal, E. "PTSD in Physically and Sexually Abused Psychiatrically Hospitalized Children." *Child Psychiatry and Human Development,* 1992, 23, 3–8.

Alexander, P. C. "Application of Attachment Theory to the Study of Sexual Abuse." *Journal of Consulting and Clinical Psychology,* 1992, 60, 185–195.

Armstrong, J. "The Psychological Organization of Multiple Personality Disordered Patients as Revealed in Psychological Testing." *Psychiatric Clinics of North America,* 1991, 14, 533–546.

Bene, E., and Anthony, J. *Manual for the Children's Version of the Family Relations Test.* Windsor, England: NFER Publishing Company, 1976.

Bretherton, I., Ridgeway, D., and Cassidy, J. "Assessing Internal Working Models of the Attachment Relationship: An Attachment Story Completion Task for 3-Year-Olds." In M. T. Greenberg, D. Cicchetti, and E. M. Cummings (eds.), *Attachment in the Preschool Years.* Chicago: University of Chicago Press, 1990.

Briere, J. "Methodological Issues in the Study of Sexual Abuse Effects." *Journal of Consulting and Clinical Psychology,* 1992, 60, 196–203.

Briere, J. *Professional Manual for the Trauma Symptom Checklist for Children.* Odessa, Fla.: Psychological Assessment Resources, in press a.

Briere, J. *Professional Manual for the Trauma Symptom Inventory.* Odessa, Fla.: Psychological Assessment Resources, in press b.

Briere, J., and Runtz, M. "Childhood Sexual Abuse: Long-Term Sequelae and Implications for Psychological Assessment." *Journal of Interpersonal Violence,* 1993, 8, 312–330.

Burkett, L. P. "Parenting Behaviors of Women Who Were Sexually Abused in Their Families of Origin." *Family Process,* 1991, 30, 421–434.

Burns, R. C., and Kaufman, S. H. *Actions, Styles and Symbols in Kinetic Family Drawings (KFD).* New York: Brunner/Mazel, 1972.

Chantler, L., Pelco, L., and Mertin, P. "Psychological Evaluation of Child Sexual Abuse Using the Louisville Behavior Checklist and Human Figure Drawing." *Child Abuse and Neglect,* 1993, 17, 271–279.

Elliott, D. M., and Briere, J. "Forensic Sexual Abuse Evaluations of Older Children: Disclosures and Symptomatology." *Behavioral Sciences and the Law,* 1994, 12, 261–277.

Everson, M. D., Hunter, W. M., Runyon, D. K., Edelsohn, G. A., and Coulter, M. L. "Maternal Support Following Disclosure of Incest." *American Journal of Orthopsychiatry,* 1989, 59, 197–207.

Exner, J. E. *The Rorschach: A Comprehensive System.* Vol. 1. New York: Wiley, 1974.

Friedrich, W. N. "Behavior Problems in Sexually Abused Children: An Adaptational Perspective." In G. E. Wyatt and G. J. Powell (eds.), *Lasting Effects of Child Sexual Abuse.* Newbury Park, Calif.: Sage, 1988.

Friedrich, W. N. *Psychotherapy of Sexually Abused Children and Their Families.* New York: W. W. Norton, 1990.

Friedrich, W. N. "Mothers of Sexually Abused Children: An MMPI Study." *Journal of Clinical Psychology,* 1991, 47, 778–783.

Friedrich W. N. "Sexual Behavior in Sexually Abused Children." *Violence Update*, 1993, *3* (5), 1–4, 7–10.

Friedrich, W. N. "Update on Clinical Assessment of Sexually Abused Children." Paper presented at the annual convention of the American Psychological Association, Los Angeles, Aug. 12, 1994a.

Friedrich, W. N. "Usefulness of Psychological Measurements in the Care of the Child." Paper presented at the San Diego Conference on Responding to Child Maltreatment, Jan. 27, 1994b.

Friedrich, W. N. "Psychotherapy of Abused Children." In J. Briere, L. Berliner, J. Bulkley, C. Jenny, and T. Reid (eds.), *APSAC Handbook on Child Maltreatment*. Newbury Park, Calif.: Sage, in press.

Friedrich, W. N., Einbender, A. J., and McCarthy, P. M. "Differences Between Sexually Abused and Nonabused Girls on the Rorschach." Unpublished manuscript, 1994.

Friedrich, W. N., Grambsch, P., Damon, L., Hewitt, S. K., Koverola, C., Lang, R. A., Wolfe, V., and Broughton, D. "Child Sexual Behavior Inventory: Normative and Clinical Comparisons." *Psychological Assessment*, 1992, *4*, 303–311.

Friedrich, W. N., Jaworski, T. M., Huxsahl, J., and Bengston, B. "Assessment of Dissociative and Sexual Behaviors in Children and Adolescents." Unpublished manuscript, 1994.

Friedrich, W. N., and Reams, R. A. "The Parentification of Children Scale." Unpublished manuscript, Mayo Clinic, Rochester, Minn., 1993.

Friedrich, W. N., and Schafer, L. "Somatic Symptoms in Sexually Abused Children." *Journal of Pediatric Psychology*, in press.

Friedrich, W. N., and Share, M. "Differences Between Sexually Abused and Nonsexually Abused Children on the Roberts Apperception Test for Children." Unpublished manuscript, 1994.

Hanson, R. F., Saunders, B. E., Lipovsky, J. A. "The Relationship Between Self-Reported Levels of Distress of Parents and Victims in Incest Families." *Journal of Child Sexual Abuse*, 1992, *1* (2), 49–60.

Hernandez, J. T. "Substance Abuse Among Sexually Abused Adolescents and Their Families." *Journal of Adolescent Health*, 1992, *13*, 658–662.

Hussey, D. L., and Singer, M. "Psychological Distress, Problem Behaviors, and Family Functioning of Sexually Abused Adolescent Inpatients." *Journal of the American Academy of Child and Adolescent Psychiatry*, 1993, *32*, 954–961.

Hussey, D. L., Strom, G., and Singer, M. I. "Male Victims of Sexual Abuse: An Analysis of Adolescent Psychiatric Inpatients." *Child and Adolescent Social Work Journal*, 1992, *9*, 491–503.

Kendall-Tackett, K. A., Williams, L. M., and Finkelhor, D. "Impact of Sexual Abuse on Children: A Review and Synthesis of Recent Empirical Studies." *Psychological Bulletin*, 1993, *113*, 164–180.

Lamb, M. E., Sternberg, K. J., and Esplin, P. W. "Factors Influencing the Reliability and Validity of Statements Made by Young Victims of Sexual Maltreatment." *Journal of Applied Developmental Psychology*, in press.

Lipovsky, J. A., Saunders, B. E., and Hanson, R. F. "Parent-Child Relationships of Victims and Siblings in Incest Families." *Journal of Child Sexual Abuse*, 1992, *1* (4), 35–49.

Loevinger, J., Wessler, R., and Redmore, C. *Measuring Ego Development.* Vol. 1: *Construction and Use of a Sentence Completion Test.* San Francisco: Jossey-Bass, 1970.

McArthur, D. S., and Roberts, G. E. *Roberts Apperception Test for Children.* Los Angeles: Western Psychological Services, 1982.

McLeer, S. V., Deblinger, E. B., Henry, D., and Orvaschel, H. "Sexually Abused Children at High Risk for Post-Traumatic Stress Disorder." *Journal of the American Academy of Child and Adolescent Psychiatry*, 1992, *31*, 875–879.

Main, M., and Hesse, E. "Parents' Unresolved Traumatic Experiences Are Related to Infant Disorganized Status." In M. T. Greenberg, D. Cicchetti, and E. M. Cummings (eds.), *Attachment in the Preschool Years*. Chicago: University of Chicago Press, 1990.

Malinosky-Rummell, R. R., and Hoier, T. S. "Validating Measures of Dissociation in Sexually Abused and Nonabused Children." *Behavioral Assessment,* 1991, *13,* 341–457.

Mannarino, A. P., Cohen, J. A., and Berman, S. R. "The Children's Attributions and Perceptions Scale: A New Measure of Sexual Abuse-Related Factors." *Journal of Clinical Child Psychology,* 1994, *23,* 204–211.

Marquardt, R., and Friedrich, W. N. "Sexual Meaning, Sexual Practices, and Body Image in Sexually Abused Adolescents." Unpublished manuscript, 1994.

Moos, R. H. *Family Environment Scale.* Palo Alto, Calif.: Consulting Psychologists Press, 1974.

Newberger, C. M., Geremy, I. M., Waternaux, C. M., and Newberger, E. H. "Mothers of Sexually Abused Children: Trauma and Repair in Longitudinal Perspective." *American Journal of Orthopsychiatry,* 1993, *63,* 92–102.

Putnam, F. W., Helmers, K., and Trickett, P. K. "Development, Reliability, and Validity of a Child Dissociation Scale." *Child Abuse and Neglect,* 1993, *17,* 731–741.

Sternberg, K. J., Lamb, M. E., Greenbaum, C., and Cicchetti, D. "Effects of Domestic Violence on Children's Behavior Problems and Depression." *Developmental Psychology,* 1993, *29,* 44–52.

Stewart, M. S., Bussey, K., Goodman, G. S., and Saywitz, K. J. "Implications of Developmental Research for Interviewing Children." *Child Abuse and Neglect,* 1993, *17,* 25–37.

Wolfe, V. V., and Gentile, C. "Psychological Assessment of Sexually Abused Children." In W. T. O'Donohue and J. H. Geer (eds.), *The Sexual Abuse of Children.* Hillsdale, N.J.: Erlbaum, 1993.

Wolfe, V. V., Gentile, C., Michienzi, T., Sas, L., and Wolfe, D. "The Children's Impact of Traumatic Events Scale: A Measure of Post-Sexual Abuse PTSD Symptoms." *Behavioral Assessment,* 1991.

Wolfe, V., and Wolfe, D. *The Sexual Abuse Fear Evaluation (SAFE): A Subscale for the Fear Survey for Children—Revised.* Unpublished questionnaire, Children's Hospital of Western Ontario, London, Canada, 1986.

Wolfe, V., Wolfe, D., and LaRose, L. *The Children's Impact of Traumatic Events Scale.* Unpublished manuscript, University of Western Ontario, 1986.

WILLIAM N. FRIEDRICH, Ph.D., is professor of psychiatry and psychology at the Mayo Medical School and consultant at the Mayo Clinic, Rochester, Minnesota.

Empirical research demonstrates a relationship between history of child sexual abuse and numerous psychological, interpersonal, and behavioral problems in adults. Long-term correlates and theoretical conceptualizations of these sequelae are described.

Long-Term Correlates of Childhood Sexual Abuse in Adult Survivors

Debra A. Neumann

Childhood sexual abuse (CSA) is increasingly recognized as a relatively common experience for both female and male children in our society. Studies that have investigated the recall of abusive childhood sexual experiences among community samples have found that one in four women and one in six men report such a history (Finkelhor, Hotaling, Lewis, and Smith, 1990). Russell (1986) surveyed the prevalence of childhood sexual victimization among adult females. When CSA was defined as involving some form of physical sexual contact by someone at least three years older before the victim reaches eighteen years of age, and was assessed in direct interviews by trained and sensitive personnel, approximately 40 percent of women surveyed reported a history of CSA. When the definition of CSA was narrowed to assess abuse perpetrated by a member of the victim's family, the rate dropped to around 19 percent and, when narrowed further to include only cases of father-daughter incest involving a biological father or stepfather, the prevalence rate was approximately 5 percent.

Among samples of women seeking psychiatric or psychological services, the reported rates are quite high; 35–50 percent of adult females who are in outpatient psychotherapy and 70 percent of women seeking psychiatric emergency services report a history of CSA (Briere, 1989; Briere and Zaidi, 1989). In addition, among specific groups the rates are consistently elevated. For example, there is an association between history of child sexual abuse and psychiatric diagnoses such as multiple personality disorder (Coons and Milstein, 1986), borderline personality disorder (Herman, Perry, and van der Kolk, 1989), or eating disorders (Steiger and Zanko, 1990). High rates of child sexual victimization are also found among chronic pelvic pain patients (Walker and others, 1988), prostitutes (Bagley and Young, 1987), substance abusers (Rosehnow, Corbett, and Devine, 1988), and homeless women (Browne, 1993).

Interest in the psychological aftermath of childhood sexual victimization has ebbed and flowed across the years. (See Herman, 1992, for a historical overview of the episodic amnesia surrounding this topic.) As interest in the topic has waxed and waned, so too has the awareness among researchers, clinicians, and the general public that CSA may be associated with negative psychological outcomes.

Initial research in this area tended to support the notion that childhood sexual contact with adults is not harmful and, in fact, may be beneficial (Bender and Blau, 1937; Bender and Grugett, 1952). However, by the 1970s, the accumulation of numerous case studies suggesting that CSA was associated with psychological problems in adult women led to intensive empirical investigation. This empirical research provided a preponderance of evidence that numerous psychological difficulties are correlated with CSA. The literature on these sequelae has been reviewed qualitatively by Beitchman and others (1992) and Browne and Finkelhor (1986), and quantitatively in a meta-analytic review by Neumann, Houskamp, Pollock, and Briere (1993).

Although not all survivors of CSA evidence long-term negative psychological outcomes, Finkelhor (1988) reported that 20–50 percent of all adult survivors have identifiable mental health impairments. Using data from the Los Angeles Epidemiological Catchment Area Study, Stein and others (1988) found that 64 percent of the women in their sample who reported a history of child sexual abuse had received a psychiatric diagnosis at some point in their lives, compared with 29 percent of women without a history of CSA. Seventy-five percent of the abused women reported at least one lifetime negative emotional reaction and 20 percent were currently experiencing such a reaction.

Research indicates that males with a history of child sexual abuse may also exhibit long-term negative psychological sequelae, although to date most empirical research using comparison groups has focused on women. In a study examining the correlates of CSA in groups of abused men and women, Briere, Evans, Runtz, and Wall (1988) found similar sequelae across sex. Kelly (1994) compared groups of abused and nonabused men and reports increased sexual identity confusion and insecurity about masculine roles in the sexually victimized group.

In the remainder of this chapter, I summarize recent theoretical developments that enable us to understand the legacy of CSA in adults. I then give an overview of symptoms that may be found in the adult survivor. This overview is organized according to a synthesis of theoretical contributions.

Theoretical Contributions

Most research to date has not been theory-based. Researchers have been interested in describing the impact of abuse. Perhaps the most important contribution to our understanding of the long-term sequelae of child sexual abuse over the past several years has been in the area of model construction and theory building. The following section summarizes the major contributions.

Traumagenic Dynamics. Finkelhor and Browne (1985) proposed a traumagenic dynamics model. According to this model, four factors associated with child sexual abuse may result in long-term negative outcomes in adult interpersonal relationships and in the ways in which adult survivors perceive themselves. These traumagenic factors are traumatic sexualization, betrayal, powerlessness, and stigmatization. Their occurrence in CSA is thought to alter the victim's self-concept, world view, and emotional capacity in a unique way, thus differentiating the long-term sequelae of CSA from those associated with other childhood trauma. Finkelhor and Browne posit that as child victims mature, their behavioral and emotional problems reflect the distortions brought about in their developing personalities by attempts to cope with the dynamics of sexual abuse.

Negative Core Effects. Briere (1989) has conceptualized the negative cognitive, interpersonal, and emotional symptomatology found in adult survivors as related to six underlying dynamics, all of which are direct outcomes of the sexual abuse experience: other-directedness, chronic perceptions of danger, self-hatred, a sense of "negative specialness," the establishment of a conditional reality based on dissociative phenomena and impaired self-reference, and heightened capacity to avoid, deny, and repress. Each of these is viewed as an adaptation to the traumatic interruption of normal childhood development brought about by sexual abuse. These adaptations generalize and become more elaborate over time.

Trauma and Affect. Psychoanalytic thinkers have also posited theoretical explanations for the psychological impact of child sexual abuse. One of these is Krystal's (1988) trauma and affect model. Krystal concluded that a trauma such as child sexual abuse entails a paralyzing, overwhelming affective state. The outcome of this state is characterized by immobilization, withdrawal, possible derealization, and evidence of psychic disorganization. Immediately after the event there is likely to be a regression in cognitive and affective functioning, followed by recuperative attempts that can be seen in the tendency to repeat (repetition compulsion), recurrent dreams, and neurotic, characterological, or psychosomatic syndromes.

Constructivist Self-Development Theory. Constructivist self-development theory (CSDT) provides a framework for understanding the impact of psychological trauma on personality development and identity (McCann and Pearlman, 1990). Three major components of the self are affected by CSA: the self capacities, which include the ability to maintain a positive sense of self, to manage and tolerate affect, and to maintain an inner sense of connection with others; frame of reference, which includes one's world view, sense of identity, and spirituality; and ego resources, which include abilities to strive for personal growth, to view oneself and others from more than one perspective, to make self-protective judgments, and to establish appropriate boundaries. In addition, the theory suggests five psychological need areas likely to be disrupted in survivors: safety, trust and dependency, esteem, control, and intimacy.

Long-Term Correlates

These theoretical constructions all posit a way of understanding the sequelae of CSA. They all view the phenomena that follow CSA as valid attempts to cope or make sense of the abuse by the survivor. These are adaptive at the time, but over time they become dysfunctional. There are theoretical commonalities in all the views noted above. For example, all theorists view CSA as an overwhelming experience that is disruptive to affective functioning and to relationships with, feelings toward, and beliefs about oneself, others, and the nature of the external world. The discussion of the long-term symptom groupings that follow is based on these commonalities. The symptoms are grouped in the following categories: affective disruptions, interpersonal disturbances, distorted self-perceptions, altered frame of reference, and behavioral adaptations. Although grouping symptoms in this manner serves a heuristic purpose, it must be stressed that the symptoms found in adult survivors of child sexual abuse represent adaptations made by them to an intolerable event and involve their own unique manner of construing that event. There is no isomorphic correspondence between category and symptom for each individual.

Affective Disruptions. One noteworthy characteristic that may be found in individuals who have suffered CSA is their incapacity to manage and tolerate strong affect. They may alternately deny or avoid strong affect or be flooded with affect intrusions. Such numbing and reexperiencing of affect may be one component of posttraumatic stress responses found in survivors (Lindberg and Distad, 1985). The affects most troublesome to survivors appear to be anger (Bryer, Nelson, Miller, and Krol, 1987), anxiety (Briere and Runtz, 1988), and depression (Peters, 1988). Some methods used to cope with overwhelming affect are dissociative defenses (Chu and Dill, 1990), obsessions and compulsions (Greenwald, Leitenberg, Cado, and Tarran, 1990), and somaticization (Springs and Friedrich, 1992).

Interpersonal Disturbances. Numerous studies point to a high correlation between history of CSA and difficulties establishing and maintaining intimate relationships in adulthood. These problems include difficulty trusting others (Gold, 1986) and social isolation and feeling inadequate in social adjustment (Harter, Alexander, and Niemeyer, 1988). Not surprisingly, one common outcome of child sexual abuse is a disruption of sexual expression, including difficulties experiencing arousal and orgasm, avoidance of sex, promiscuity, and a general feeling of sexual dissatisfaction (Tsai, Feldman-Summers, and Edgar, 1979). Survivors of CSA also have a tendency to be revictimized in adulthood. For example, they may be sexually revictimized by rape or in a battering relationship (Wyatt, Guthrie, and Notgrass, 1992).

Distorted Self-Perceptions. Among distortions cited here are intense self-loathing (Briere, 1989), poor self-esteem (Bagley and Ramsay, 1986), severe self-criticism, guilt, and perceived undeservingness (Briere and Runtz, 1990), and shame (Courtois, 1979). Some research suggests that the impairment in self-perception may be related to age or developmental level at the time of onset of CSA, with younger victims suffering more severe negative effects in this area (Zivney, Nash, and Hulsey, 1988).

Altered Frame of Reference. Janoff-Bulman (1992) describes the disruptive impact of traumatic events on the world views, assumptions, and sense of identity of survivors. Sargeant (1989) has noted that victims of intrafamilial abuse are often unable to find solace in personal images of their deities. It also appears that female survivors may have difficulty integrating femininity into their sense of identity (Saakvitne, 1992). Beitchman and others (1992) noted a possible association between CSA history and homosexual activity, suggesting that there may be a relationship between abuse and adult sexual orientation.

Behavioral Adaptations. Several behaviors frequently occur among survivors of CSA that do not fit neatly in any of these categories. They may express any or all of the disruptions noted above. These include suicidality (Briere and Runtz, 1986), self-mutilation (Shapiro, 1987), and substance abuse (Swett and others, 1991).

The sequelae noted above are thought to represent an adaptive attempt by survivors to create and maintain a sense of self. This has two primary implications for professionals working with survivors. First, common symptoms may have diverse etiologies and functions. Second, focused interventions must be individualized, based on the meaning of the symptom for each survivor.

Moderating and Mediating Variables

CSA and its sequelae do not occur in a vacuum. There is a striking need for investigation of the role of moderating and mediating variables in the long-term outcome of a childhood history of sexual abuse. In the next section, I consider three such variables—the family context, locus of abuse, and degree of violence—and examine some factors that may contribute to resiliency in survivors.

Family Context. Attempts have been made to statistically investigate the role of family dynamics as moderating abuse-associated outcomes. A key question here concerns the specificity of symptoms to CSA. Are the sequelae primarily related to the abuse or to the dynamics of the victim's family? Briere and Elliott (1993), while questioning current statistical approaches to controlling family effects in abuse research, cite instances where the abuse-symptom relationships remain in some form despite third variable control (for example, Peters, 1988). This suggests that although the family context of abuse is important, abuse itself plays a key role in the etiology of sequelae.

A second question of interest is the extent to which positive family context moderates abuse sequelae. There is some evidence that maternal support can be an important moderator, alleviating some symptomatology (Peters, 1988; Marvasti, 1993).

Locus of Abuse. It is a common clinical hypothesis that intrafamilial CSA sequelae differ from those of extrafamilial abuse (Harter, Alexander, and Niemeyer, 1988). Some studies suggest that abuse perpetrated by parents or immediate family members is more harmful than abuse by those at greater distance from the child (Briere and Elliott, 1993; Tsai, Feldman-Summers, and Edgar, 1979; Russell, 1986). Neumann, Houskamp, Pollock, and Briere (1993) found a moderately strong symptom-locus relationship when comparing sequelae in survivors of intrafamilial versus extrafamilial abuse. The result suggested greater symptomatology among survivors of intrafamilial abuse. However, this finding was based on only eight studies and must be interpreted with caution. Others suggest that it is the meaning and context of the relationship between perpetrator and victim that moderates outcomes, rather than familial locus per se (Laurie Anne Pearlman, personal communication, 1993).

Degree of Violence. The trauma and victimization literature suggests that symptom development subsequent to violent crime, rape, or combat trauma is mediated by the degree and intensity of traumatic violence of the event (Foy, Sipprelle, Rueger, and Carroll, 1984; Kilpatrick and others, 1989). There is some evidence that more serious psychological aftermaths are associated with brutal, bizarre, and sadistic abuse and with abuse of longer duration. For example, Briere (1988) investigated the relationship between six abuse characteristics (duration, concomitant physical abuse, parental incest, completed intercourse, lifetime number of perpetrators, and bizarreness) and psychological problems in a clinical group of adult female survivors. He found that as the magnitude of violence in the abuse experience increased, the magnitude of psychological problems reported in adulthood also increased. Other investigators have noted the frequent co-occurrence of repetitive, severe, and sadistic child sexual abuse and adult multiple personality disorder diagnoses (Putnam, 1989).

Resiliency. Not all sexually victimized children evidence psychological problems as adults. Children often exhibit significant resilience and may be able, given the right temperament and a supportive environment, to overcome childhood adversity with a minimum of disruptions in adulthood (Rutter, 1985). Garmezy (1991) suggests that positive temperament, a supportive family, and social support are important factors that contribute to resiliency. Holman and Silver (1993) found that among adult survivors of incest, resilience and adaptive outcomes are related to the use of behaviors that decrease social isolation and increase the possibility of receiving social support, having expressed hostile feelings about their abuse in the past, and the ability to separate past from present and maintain a focus on the present. In addition, Pearlman and colleagues suggest that survivors of CSA may be quite high-functioning, even "super-competent" (in the words of CSDT, they have strong ego resources), and this adaptiveness may mask disrupted self-capacities, an inner sense of being flawed, or significant depression (Gelinas, 1983).

Conclusion

Child sexual abuse is thought to involve a disruption of the core person, often eventuating in affect tolerance difficulties, painful perceptions of self, problems in interpersonal relationships, and disrupted beliefs about oneself and the external world. Empirical research has established significant differences between groups of adult CSA survivors and nonsurvivors, including anger, anxiety, depression, dissociation, interpersonal problems, obsessions and compulsions, posttraumatic stress responses, revictimization, poor self-concept, self-mutilation, sexual problems, poor somatization, substance abuse, and suicidality. Although the research demonstrates significant associations between childhood history and long-term symptomatology, these findings are vulnerable to criticism based on retrospective, correlational methods (Briere and Elliott, 1993). Using such research methods, we cannot rule out the effects of recall bias on reports of history, nor can we affirm a causal relationship between childhood event and adult outcome. The associations found in these studies may represent the correlation of both CSA and adult outcome with a common third factor, such as other types of childhood abuse or stressors occurring across the life span.

In order to clarify the relationships noted thus far, a new research paradigm is needed. Ideally, this research will be theory-based and longitudinal. Although few longitudinal studies are available to date, Egeland and colleagues have followed a cohort of abused children from early in life into midchildhood and have documented a number of negative psychological symptoms in these children as they mature (Egeland, 1989; Egeland and Erickson, 1987; Egeland and Faber, 1984). If additional longitudinal research replicates these findings, we can assert that sexual abuse plays a key, but not singular, role in long-term negative sequelae in adult survivors.

References

Bagley, C., and Ramsay, R. "Sexual Abuse in Childhood: Psychosocial Outcomes and Implications for Social Work Practice." *Journal of Social Work and Human Sexuality*, 1986, *4*, 33–48.

Bagley, C., and Young, L. "Juvenile Prostitution and Child Sexual Abuse: A Controlled Study." *Canadian Journal of Community Mental Health*, 1987, *6*, 5–26.

Beitchman, J. H., Zucker, K. J., Hood, J. E., daCosta, G. A., Akman, D., and Cassavia, E. "A Review of the Long-Term Effects of Child Sexual Abuse." *Child Abuse and Neglect*, 1992, *16*, 101–118.

Bender, L., and Blau, A. "The Reaction of Children to Sexual Relations with Adults." *American Journal of Orthopsychiatry*, 1937, 7, 500–518.

Bender, L., and Grugett, A. "A Follow-up Report on Children Who Had Atypical Sexual Experiences." *American Journal of Orthopsychiatry*, 1952, 22, 825–837.

Briere, J. "The Long-Term Clinical Correlates of Childhood Sexual Victimization." *Annals of the New York Academy of Sciences*, 1988, 528, 327–334.

Briere, J. *Therapy for Adults Molested as Children: Beyond Survival.* New York: Springer, 1989.

Briere, J., and Elliott, D. "Sexual Abuse, Family Environment, and Psychological Symptoms: On the Validity of Statistical Control." *Journal of Consulting and Clinical Psychology*, 1993, 61 (2), 284–288.

Briere, J., Evans, D., Runtz, M., and Wall, T. "Symptomatology in Men Who Were Molested as Children: A Comparison Study." *American Journal of Orthopsychiatry*, 1988, 58 (3), 457–461.

Briere, J., and Runtz, M. "Suicidal Thoughts and Behaviors in Former Sexual Abuse Victims." *Canadian Journal of Behavioral Science*, 1986, 18 (4), 413–423.

Briere, J., and Runtz, M. "Symptomatology Associated with Childhood Sexual Victimization in a Nonclinical Adult Sample." *Child Abuse and Neglect*, 1988, 12, 51–59.

Briere, J., and Runtz, M. "Differential Adult Symptomatology Associated with Three Types of Child Abuse Histories." *Child Abuse and Neglect*, 1990, 14, 357–364.

Briere, J., and Zaidi, L. Y. "Sexual Abuse Histories and Sequelae in Female Psychiatric Emergency Room Patients." *American Journal of Psychiatry*, 1989, 146 (12), 1602–1606.

Browne, A. "Family Violence and Homelessness: The Relevance of Trauma Histories in the Lives of Homeless Women." *American Journal of Orthopsychiatry*, 1993, 63 (3), 370–385.

Browne, A., and Finkelhor, D. "Impact of Child Sexual Abuse: A Review of the Research." *Psychological Bulletin*, 1986, 99 (1), 66–77.

Bryer, J. B., Nelson, B. A., Miller, J. B., and Krol, P. A. "Childhood Sexual and Physical Abuse as Factors in Adult Psychiatric Illness." *American Journal of Orthopsychiatry*, 1987, 144 (11), 1426–1430.

Chu, J. A., and Dill, D. L. "Dissociative Symptoms in Relations to Childhood Physical and Sexual Abuse." *American Journal of Psychiatry*, 1990, 147 (7), 887–892.

Coons, P. M., and Milstein, V. "Psychosexual Disturbances in Multiple Personality: Characteristics, Etiology, and Treatment." *Journal of Clinical Psychiatry*, 1986, 47, 106–110.

Courtois, C. "The Incest Experience and Its Aftermath." *Victimology*, 1979, 4, 337–347.

Egeland, B. "A Longitudinal Study of High-Risk Families: Issues and Findings." Paper presented at the Research Forum on Issues in the Longitudinal Study of Child Maltreatment, Toronto, Canada, Oct. 1989.

Egeland, B., and Erickson, M. "Psychologically Unavailable Caregiving." In M. R. Brassard, R. Germain, and S. N. Hart (eds.), *Psychological Maltreatment of Children and Youth.* Elmsford, N.Y.: Pergamon Press, 1987.

Egeland, B., and Faber, E. "Infant-Mother Attachment: Factors Related to Its Development and Changes over Time." *Child Development*, 1984, 55, 753–771.

Finkelhor, D. "The Trauma of Childhood Sexual Abuse: Two Models." In G. E. Wyatt and G. J. Powell (eds.), *Lasting Effects of Child Sexual Abuse.* Newbury Park, Calif.: Sage, 1988.

Finkelhor, D., and Browne, A. "The Traumatic Impact of Child Sexual Abuse: A Conceptualization." *American Journal of Orthopsychiatry*, 1985, 55, 530–541.

Finkelhor, D., Hotaling, G., Lewis, I. A., and Smith, C. "Sexual Abuse in a National Survey of Adult Men and Women: Prevalence, Characteristics, and Risk Factors." *Child Abuse and Neglect*, 1990, 14, 19–28.

Foy, D. W., Sipprelle, R. C., Rueger, D. B., and Carroll, E. "Etiology of Posttraumatic Stress Disorder in Vietnam Veterans: Analysis of Premilitary, Military, and Combat Exposure Influences." *Journal of Consulting and Clinical Psychology*, 1984, 52, 79–87.

Garmezy, N. "Resilience in Children's Adaptation to Negative Life Events and Stressed Environments." *Pediatric Annals*, 1991, 20, 459–465.

Gelinas, D. J. "The Persisting Negative Effects of Incest." *Psychiatry*, 1983, *46*, 312–332.

Gold, E. R. "Long-Term Effects of Sexual Victimization in Children: An Attributional Approach." *Journal of Consulting and Clinical Psychology*, 1986, *54*, 471–475.

Greenwald, E., Leitenberg, H., Cado, S., and Tarran, M. J. "Childhood Sexual Abuse: Long-Term Effects on Psychological and Sexual Functioning in a Nonclinical and Nonstudent Sample of Adult Women." *Child Abuse and Neglect*, 1990, *14*, 503–513.

Harter, S., Alexander, P. C., and Niemeyer, R. A. "Long-Term Effects of Incestuous Childhood in College Women: Social Adjustment, Social Cognition, and Family Characteristics." *Journal of Consulting and Clinical Psychology*, 1988, *56* (1), 5–8.

Herman, J. L. *Trauma and Recovery*. New York: Basic Books, 1992.

Herman, J. L., Perry, J. C., and van der Kolk, B. A. "Childhood Trauma in Borderline Personality Disorder." *American Journal of Psychiatry*, 1989, *146*, 490–495.

Holman, E. A., and Silver, R. C. "Coping with Misfortune: Resilience in Adult Survivors of Childhood Incest." Unpublished manuscript, 1993.

Janoff-Bulman, R. *Shattered Assumptions: Toward a New Psychology of Trauma*. New York: Free Press, 1992.

Kelly, R. J. "Comparing Sexually Abused and Non-Abused Men." Paper presented at the annual meeting of the American Psychological Association, Los Angeles, Aug. 1994.

Kilpatrick, D. G., Saunders, B. E., Amick-McMullen, A., Best, C. L., and Veronen, L. J. "Victim and Crime Factors Associated with the Development of Crime-Related Post-Traumatic Stress Disorder." *Behavior Therapy*, 1989, *20* (2), 199–214.

Krystal, H. *Integration and Self-Healing: Affect, Trauma, Alexithymia*. Hillsdale, N.J.: Analytic Press, 1988.

Lindberg, F. H., and Distad, L. J. "Post-Traumatic Stress Disorders in Women Who Experienced Childhood Incest." *Child Abuse and Neglect*, 1985, *9*, 329–334.

McCann, I. L., and Pearlman, L. A. *Psychological Trauma and the Adult Survivor: Theory, Therapy, and Transformation*. New York: Brunner/Mazel, 1990.

Marvasti, J. A. "Psychopathology in Adult Survivors of Incest." *American Journal of Forensic Psychiatry*, 1993, *14* (2), 61–73.

Neumann, D. A., Houskamp, B. M., Pollock, V. E., and Briere, J. "The Long-Term Sequelae of Childhood Sexual Abuse in Women: A Meta-Analytic Review." Unpublished manuscript, 1993.

Peters, S. D. "Child Sexual Abuse and Later Psychological Problems." In G. E. Wyatt and G. J. Powell (eds.), *Lasting Effects of Child Sexual Abuse*. Newbury Park, Calif.: Sage, 1988.

Putnam, F. W. *Diagnosis and Treatment of Multiple Personality Disorder*. New York: Guilford, 1989.

Rosehnow, D. J., Corbett, R., and Devine, D. "Molested as Children: A Hidden Contribution to Substance Abuse?" *Journal of Substance Abuse Treatment*, 1988, *5*, 13–18.

Russell, D.E.H. *The Secret Trauma: Incest in the Lives of Women and Children*. New York: Basic Books, 1986.

Rutter, M. "Resilience in the Face of Adversity: Protective Factors and Resistance to Psychiatric Disorder." *British Journal of Psychiatry*, 1985, *147*, 598–611.

Saakvitne, K. W. "Incest and Feminine Identity: Shame, Sexuality, and Rage." Paper presented at the annual convention of the American Psychological Association, Washington, D.C., Aug. 1992.

Sargeant, N. M. "Spirituality and Adult Survivors of Child Sexual Abuse: Some Treatment Issues." In S. S. Sgroi (ed.), *Vulnerable Populations*. Vol. 2. Lexington, Mass.: Lexington Books, 1989.

Shapiro, S. "Mutilation and Self-Blame in Incest Victims." *American Journal of Psychotherapy*, 1987, *41*, 46–54.

Springs, F. E., and Friedrich, W. N. "Health Risk Behaviors and Medical Sequelae of Childhood Sexual Abuse." *Mayo Clinic Proceedings*, 1992, *67*, 527–532.

Steiger, H., and Zanko, M. "Sexual Traumata Among Eating Disordered, Psychiatric, and Normal Female Groups." *Journal of Interpersonal Violence,* 1990, *5,* 74–86.

Stein, J. A., Golding, J. M., Siegel, J. M., Burnham, M. A., and Sorensen, S. B. "Long-Term Sequelae of Child Sexual Abuse: The Los Angeles Epidemiologic Catchment Area Study." In G. E. Wyatt and G. J. Powell (eds.), *Lasting Effects of Child Sexual Abuse.* Newbury Park, Calif.: Sage, 1988.

Swett, C., Cohen, C., Surrey, J., Compaine, A., and Chavez, R. "High Rates of Alcohol Use and History of Physical and Sexual Abuse Among Women Outpatients." *American Journal of Drug and Alcohol Abuse,* 1991, *17* (1), 49–60.

Tsai, M., Feldman-Summers, S., and Edgar, M. "Childhood Molestation: Variables Related to Differential Impacts on Psychosexual Functioning in Adult Women." *Journal of Abnormal Psychology,* 1979, *88,* 407–417.

Walker, E., Katon, W., Harrop-Griffiths, J., Holm, L., Russo, J., and Hickok, L. R. "Relationship of Chronic Pelvic Pain to Psychiatric Diagnoses and Child Sexual Abuse." *American Journal of Psychiatry,* 1988, *145* (1), 75–79.

Wyatt, G. E., Guthrie, D., and Notgrass, C. M. "Differential Effects of Women's Child Sexual Abuse and Subsequent Sexual Victimization." *Journal of Consulting and Clinical Psychology,* 1992, *60* (2), 167–173.

Zivney, O. A., Nash, M. R., and Hulsey, T. L. "Sexual Abuse in Early Versus Late Childhood: Differing Patterns of Pathology as Revealed on the Rorschach." *Psychotherapy,* 1988, *25,* 99–106.

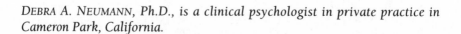

DEBRA A. NEUMANN, Ph.D., is a clinical psychologist in private practice in Cameron Park, California.

Symptom manifestations of posttraumatic stress disorder (PTSD) are explained in light of current research findings. Assessment methods for evaluating PTSD and trauma exposure are presented and implications for treatment are discussed.

Posttraumatic Stress Disorder in Victimization-Related Traumata

Millie C. Astin, Christopher M. Layne, Angela J. Camilleri, David W. Foy

Posttraumatic stress disorder (PTSD) is a diagnostic category used to describe a pattern of symptoms that may develop in individuals who have experienced traumatic stressors, including violent victimization. Although many of the symptoms of PTSD had previously been recognized, PTSD became an official diagnosis in 1980 with the advent of DSM-III (American Psychiatric Association, 1980). This category was derived largely from the study of combat veterans, but since then has been applied to a wide range of trauma groups including survivors of rape, childhood sexual abuse, physical abuse (including battering), criminal victimization, and natural and artificial disasters.

To qualify for a diagnosis of PTSD according to DSM-IV, the individual must have experienced, witnessed, or otherwise been confronted with an event that involved actual or threatened death, serious injury, or threat to physical integrity. Second, the individual's response to the event must include intense fear, helplessness, or horror. Thus, an event is defined as traumatic when it has involved death or serious injury or the threat of death or injury *and* the individual experiences strong negative affect in response to the event. In earlier versions of DSM, a traumatic event was defined as "an event outside the range of usual human experience that would be markedly distressing to almost anyone." With this earlier definition, a traumatic stressor had to be relatively rare and "most people" would have to find it disturbing. The utility of the criterion "outside the range of usual human experience" was debated because many victim-related traumas such as rape, sexual abuse, and battering are relatively common experiences for women and children. DSM-IV's definition eliminates this problem and emphasizes that the direct or indirect threat to life or well-being and how an individual responds to that threat are specifically what makes a given event traumatic.

Symptoms

Symptom manifestations fall into three broad categories. These include intrusive symptoms, avoidance and detachment symptoms, and symptoms of physiological hyperarousal. With intrusion symptoms, the traumatic event is reexperienced in some fashion. These may include intrusive memories in the waking state in the form of flashbacks or intensely vivid reenactment experiences in which the original traumatic fear and psychological distress are also reactivated. Intrusion patterns may also occur during the sleeping state in the form of thematically related nightmares. Additionally, when faced with cues associated with the traumatic event, whether actual or symbolic, the individual may exhibit physiological responses such as increased heart rate, perspiration, and rapid breathing. All of these phenomena are generally experienced as distressing and intrusive because the individual has little control over when or how they occur and because they elicit the negative emotions associated with the initial victimization experience (Janoff-Bulman, 1992; Resick and Schnicke, 1992).

Avoidance and detachment symptoms reflect the individual's attempt to gain psychological and emotional distance from the trauma. Avoidance (or escape) patterns may be observed when trauma victims show discomfort followed by shifting attention away from reminders of their traumatic experiences. Thus, the individual tries to avoid thoughts and feelings about the trauma, avoids situations and events reminiscent of the trauma, and may actually forget significant aspects of the trauma. Successful efforts to avoid painful reminders by eliminating risk of exposure to them may be learned through negative reinforcement. This may become a pervasive behavioral response resulting in detachment from all emotions, both positive and negative. This, of course, may interfere profoundly with the individual's ability to relate to others, enjoy daily life, remain productive, and plan for the future. Intuitively, one might expect that these symptoms reflect a direct attempt to distance oneself from the actual traumatic event. Others more recently have suggested that avoidance symptoms are a response to intrusive symptomatology (Creamer, Burgess, and Pattison, 1992). Intrusive symptoms are generally experienced as extremely aversive because they elicit the negative affect associated with the trauma, and thus, the individual avoids all reminders of the traumatic event in order to diminish exposure to cues that trigger intrusive memories. Similarly, detachment or numbing symptoms are an attempt to cut off the aversive feelings associated with intrusive memories (Resick and Schnicke, 1992). Avoidance of trauma-related cues may come to characterize the lifestyles of survivors who are unable to successfully overcome their immediate trauma crisis reactions. Feared stimuli eliciting escape or avoidance responses may not be limited to the physical environment. Strong negative emotions such as rage, grief, and intense anxiety or panic may elicit patterns of response very similar to the individual's original trauma reactions (reenactment), thereby establishing escape or avoidant behaviors in a much wider range of situations.

Symptoms of increased physiological arousal suggest that the individual is in a constant state of "fight or flight," which is similar to how the individual's body responded during the actual traumatic event. In this constant state of alert, the individual is primed to react to new threats of danger even in relatively safe situations. During a crisis, this response is adaptive because it facilitates survival. However, as a steady state, hyperarousal interferes with daily functioning. In this state, the individual spends a great deal of energy scanning the environment for danger cues (hypervigilance). The individual is likely to exhibit sleep disturbance, decreased concentration, irritability, and an overreactivity to stimuli (exaggerated startle response). There is evidence to suggest that this constant state of tension has deleterious effects on overall physical health, as evidenced by increased health problems in individuals with chronic PTSD (Kulka and others, 1990). Autonomic arousal on presentation of trauma-related cues is consistently found among combat veterans for approximately two-thirds of PTSD-positive subjects. Other trauma populations have also reported hypervigilance, exaggerated startle responses, and panic symptoms.

In addition to classic symptom patterns of intrusion, avoidance, and hyperarousal, cognitive distortions indicative of shattered life assumptions are also frequently observed (Janoff-Bulman, 1992). Critical assumptions about personal invulnerability, equitability and fairness of life, and personal self-worth may shift radically after traumatic victimization. Extreme self-blame, inability to trust others, and constant fear for personal safety may develop to the extent that survivors are rarely free of the need to constantly monitor their interpersonal and physical environments for signs of danger.

Diagnostic Issues

A number of diagnostic issues, many representing changes between DSM-III-R and DSM-IV, complicate the assessment and treatment of trauma victims. These include diagnostic criteria, longitudinal course, partial PTSD, and comorbidity.

DSM Criteria. Consistent with earlier versions, DSM-IV criteria require one intrusion symptom, three avoidance symptoms, and two hyperarousal symptoms that last for at least one month before a diagnosis of PTSD can be made. Some shifting between categories has taken place in DSM-IV with one Category D hyperarousal symptom (physiological reactivity when exposed to reminders of the trauma) having moved to Category B (intrusion).

Longitudinal Course. Research suggests that the one-month criterion as well as the criteria for number of intrusion, avoidance, and hyperarousal symptoms may be questionable. A substantial proportion of trauma survivors exhibit symptoms of PTSD immediately after the traumatic event. These rates drop almost by half within three months post-trauma, but then tend to stabilize. For example, rape survivors assessed at two weeks, one month, three months, six months, and nine months exhibited PTSD rates of 94 percent, 65 percent, 47 percent, 41.7 percent, and 41.7 percent respectively (Olasov Rothbaum and Foa, 1993). Thus, after three months, PTSD rates did not drop substantially. Similar findings have been observed in various trauma groups (Kilpatrick and others, 1987). Although some researchers recommended that a three-month duration of symptoms be incorporated into DSM-IV because this cutoff may more accurately predict a chronic course of PTSD (Olasov Rothbaum and Foa, 1993), the one-month criterion was maintained in DSM-IV. It should be noted that before the three-month (recommended) or one-month (current) cutoff, individuals may exhibit a full spectrum of PTSD symptoms, but do not qualify for a diagnosis of PTSD. This is because these symptoms are expected after a traumatic event and, although distressing, do not constitute pathology per se unless they become entrenched. However, DSM-IV has introduced a new diagnosis, acute stress disorder, that includes some symptoms of PTSD in addition to dissociative and somatic symptoms. This new disorder can be used only for individuals who experience symptoms of less than one month's duration after a traumatic event and who experience disruption of the ability to function. Although the use of this diagnosis may allow for earlier intervention with trauma victims, the disadvantage is that it pathologizes symptomatology that is almost universally experienced post-trauma and that remits without intervention in many individuals.

As noted above, PTSD symptoms may spontaneously remit within the first three months post-trauma. However, if symptoms do not remit within this time frame, PTSD tends to persist over time and may worsen without appropriate intervention. Several studies of trauma survivors have demonstrated the presence of diagnosable PTSD many years after the trauma (Kilpatrick and others, 1987; Kulka and others, 1990).

Partial PTSD. Although both DSM-III-R and DSM-IV require a total of six symptoms falling into specific categories, there is some debate as to how many symptoms must be present at any one time. Some data suggest that intrusion symptoms may be more predominant soon after the trauma, whereas avoidance symptoms may be more prevalent later on (Solomon and Mikulincer, 1988). Horowitz (1986) has theorized that intrusion and avoidance symptoms may alternate in a cyclical fashion. Thus, PTSD symptoms may not fall into the discrete pattern required by DSM-III-R or DSM-IV. The implication of this is that current criteria for diagnosing PTSD may miss many individuals with PTSD if they are assessed at only one point in time. Related to this is the issue of subthreshold or partial PTSD. An individual with four or five symptoms of PTSD or one with numerous intrusion and hyperarousal symptoms but no avoidance symptoms may experience significant distress, but technically does not meet the criteria for PTSD. Kulka and colleagues (1990) found an 11 percent prevalence rate of three to five PTSD symptoms in a sample of combat veterans an average of nineteen years post-trauma. Thus, a sizeable proportion of trauma survivors may exhibit partial PTSD and may benefit from treatment. Some have suggested that partial PTSD be introduced into the nosology in order to identify such individuals, but DSM-IV criteria do not include this category.

Comorbidity. High rates of PTSD have been found in victim-related trauma survivors, but there is also a high likelihood of the presence of comorbid Axis I and Axis II disorders. Individuals with PTSD are at higher risk for developing disorders of depression, anxiety, and substance abuse (Helzer, Robins, and McEnvoy, 1987; Kulka and others, 1990). Thus, PTSD may represent only a portion of the sequelae associated with traumatic victimization. However, data suggest that at least some comorbid conditions may be directly related to the presence of PTSD. Increased substance abuse has been well-documented in trauma survivors and may represent another form of avoidance or numbing. Research on depression in persons with PTSD has demonstrated different biophysiological responses than those found in individuals with depression alone. This finding suggests that the depression that sometimes accompanies PTSD may have a different biological base than depression not associated with PTSD (Pitman, 1993). Thus, although it can be argued that trauma survivors may need to be treated for more than PTSD, it may also be true that treatment of PTSD can be crucially linked to the resolution of comorbid conditions.

Knowledge of the Disorder

Because trauma exposure rates vary across clinical and community populations, with clinical samples showing higher rates, it is important to distinguish between the types of populations sampled when prevalence rates for trauma exposure are being considered. Among the 8.2 million Vietnam era veterans, 3.14 million (38 percent) actually experienced combat exposure by virtue of assignment within the hostile fire zone (Kulka and others, 1990). Epidemiology of domestic violence has been the topic of several recent national studies in which approximately 12 percent of female respondents reported being battered by their spouses (Straus and Gelles, 1986). Sexual assault rates for females have been reported by numerous studies of both community and clinical populations. A recent community study of childhood sexual abuse conducted by Finkelhor, Hotaling, Lewis, and Smith (1990) produced a 27 percent rate for females and a 16 percent rate for males. In clinical samples, childhood sexual abuse rates are typically much higher. Briere and Runtz (1987) reported a 44 percent exposure rate in women seeking crisis counseling. In a study of women being evaluated in a medical center psychiatric emergency room, Briere and Zaidi (1989) found that 74 percent reported a history of childhood sexual abuse. Recent studies on community samples have produced findings for the prevalence of completed rape during adulthood in women ranging from 13 to 26 percent (Kilpatrick and Resnick, 1993).

Psychopathology

Disorder rates in exposed individuals vary as a function of the degree of exposure. Studies of clinical samples in our lab comparing PTSD rates in "high versus low" exposed subjects consistently show that high exposure is associated with more than twice the risk found for low-exposure in combat veterans (Foy, Resnick, Sipprelle, and Carroll, 1987), adult sexual assault survivors, (Rowan, Foy, Rodriguez, and Ryan, 1994), child sexual assault survivors (Koverola and Foy, 1993), and battered women (Houskamp and Foy, 1991). In these studies, high exposure is defined as personal victimization including both physical injury and perceived life threat.

A recent national epidemiology study conducted with a probability sample of veterans in community settings revealed a lifetime PTSD prevalence rate of 30 percent, with 15.2 percent of subjects showing a current positive diagnosis (Jordan, 1991). In our clinical samples of Vietnam combat veterans receiving services in Los Angles area Veterans' Administration (VA) medical centers, current PTSD positive diagnostic rates often exceed 50 percent (Foy and others, 1987). Although studies to establish the prevalence of PTSD in community samples of battered women have not yet been reported, clinical samples of battered women residing in shelters or attending community-based self-help groups have shown PTSD rates of 45–58 percent in two successive studies (Astin, Ogland-Hand, Coleman, and Foy, in press; Houskamp and Foy, 1991).

Studies assessing PTSD in children who have been recently sexually abused show positive diagnostic rates of approximately 50 percent (Koverola and Foy, 1993; McLeer and others, 1988). In a recent study of PTSD in a clinical sample of adult survivors of childhood sexual assault, a PTSD rate of 65 percent was obtained (Rowan, Foy, Rodriguez, and Ryan, 1994). Using nationally drawn community samples, current estimates for PTSD prevalence in adult rape victims show current rates of 13 percent and lifetime rates of 35 percent (Kilpatrick and Resnick, 1993).

Conceptual Model of PTSD

Assessment and treatment efforts can be informed by an interactive model including both environmental and individual factors that are assumed necessary for understanding the development and maintenance of PTSD symptoms. Individuals are placed at risk for the disorder when they are exposed to an overwhelming traumatic stressor. An immediate crisis emotional reaction is hypothesized as a critical link in the causal chain leading to acute distress. Whether PTSD subsequently develops is influenced by additional mediating variables from biological, psychological, and social domains.

These mediating variables may interact with the primary etiological agent (traumatic event) through several possible routes. First, the presence of some additional factors may increase risk for developing PTSD by functioning as vulnerability factors that interact with traumatic experience to heighten reactivity. Conversely, mediating factors that lower PTSD susceptibility are described as resilience or protective factors. Other factors may be influential through an indirect route in which the presence of the mediating variable increases the probability of trauma exposure.

Assessment Considerations. In keeping with the interactive emphasis of the model, heterogeneity of trauma experience is assumed so that survivors receive clinical assessment appropriate for the uniqueness of their particular trauma. Comprehensive assessment of the chronology and details of the actual trauma is vital. (See Table 4.1 for a list of trauma exposure measures that we and others have commonly used with various trauma groups.) Because critical emphasis is also placed on the nature and intensity of the immediate crisis reaction for determining the likelihood of acute PTSD, thorough assessment of the individual's affective, cognitive, and behavioral responses during the trauma is also essential. History of prior trauma exposure requires priority for comprehensive assessment. Several studies have shown that previous traumatization can be a powerful determinant of present PTSD reactivity. For example, it now appears that childhood sexual abuse increases the risk for PTSD in battered women (Astin, Ogland-Hand, Coleman, and Foy, in press).

Other potential mediating factors in biological, social, and individual domains also require attention during clinical assessment. For example, evaluating family background for history of psychological disorders and significant family dysfunction is important. Family factors, both genetic and social, may be implicated in intergenerational transmission of risk for individual psychopathology. Similarly, levels of social support and intercurrent life events, as well as other coping resources, should be evaluated in order to identify present sources of vulnerability and resiliency.

Table 4.1. Trauma Exposure Assessment Instruments

Trauma Group	Instrument	Authors
Child physical abuse	Assessing Environments III	Rausch and Knutson, 1991
Child sexual abuse	Sexual Abuse Exposure Questionnaire	Rowan, Foy, Rodriguez, and Ryan, 1994
Combat	Combat Exposure Scale	Foy, Sipprelle, Rueger, and Carroll, 1984
Community violence	Survey of Children's Exposure to Community Violence	Richters and Martinez, 1993
Marital battering	Conflict Tactic Scale	Straus, 1979
Rape	Incident Report Interview	Kilpatrick and others, 1987

Symptomatic assessment efforts should include attention to the classic features of traumatic responding: patterns of intrusion, avoidance, and arousal. Dichotomous assignment of trauma survivors to PTSD positive and negative diagnostic groups is often important for research purposes, but this procedure may impose an undesirable element of arbitrariness in some evaluations for clinical purposes. For clinical applications, it may be useful to conceptualize the number and intensity of PTSD symptoms as continuous variables in which considerable variation is to be expected across individuals. In this context, the concept of partial PTSD may be useful to describe symptom levels that are clinically relevant but fall short of meeting full diagnostic criteria.

PTSD Assessment Measures.   Structured and semistructured interviews designed to assess PTSD symptomatology are generally recommended because of their high concurrence with clinicians' diagnosis of PTSD. However, they generally require training and experience to administer accurately and consistently. Several that are used in both clinical and research applications include the Structured Clinical Interview for DSM-III-R, PTSD module (SCID-R) (Spitzer, Williams, Gibbon, and First, 1989), the Clinician-Administered PTSD Scale (CAPS) (Blake and others, 1990), and the Diagnostic Interview Schedule (DIS) (Helzer, Robins, and McEnvoy, 1987).

Paper-and-pencil self-report instruments have also been developed to assess PTSD. Although less reliable than interviews because of the tendency to underreport true cases of PTSD, self-report instruments have the advantage of being easy to administer, especially in clinical settings. Multiple measures are recommended for PTSD diagnosis and assessment to increase accuracy when using self-report measures.

Two measures often used with a variety of trauma populations are the Los Angeles Symptom Checklist (LASC) (Leskin and Foy, 1993) and the Impact of Event Scale (IES) (Horowitz, Wilner, and Alvarez, 1979). The LASC consists of forty-three distress items, which the individual rates on a five-point scale from 0 ("no problem") to 5 ("extreme problem"). A subset of seventeen items reflects DSM-III-R criteria for intrusive, avoidance and numbing, and hyperarousal symptoms. Although a PTSD diagnosis can be obtained from this instrument, the LASC also yields a cumulative score that reflects overall PTSD severity. Adolescent and adult versions are available in both English and Spanish. Norms are available for a variety of trauma populations.

The IES specifically assesses intrusion and avoidance symptoms. Respondents rate the frequency of each item experienced within the past seven days on a four-point scale from "not at all" to "often." Items are summed to yield an intrusion score and an avoidance score, which reflect severity of symptoms. This instrument has been used with a wide variety of trauma populations and has successfully distinguished some trauma groups. Its primary disadvantage is that it cannot be scored dichotomously to yield a PTSD diagnosis. A recent revision has been developed that includes items related to hyperarousal symptoms (Weiss, Marmar, Metzler, and Ronfeldt, in press).

PTSD in Children

Children's psychological reactions to various human-induced traumas, including warfare, hostage situations, sexual abuse, physical abuse, and community violence, have also been investigated from a PTSD conceptual framework. These studies have consistently documented a constellation of intrusive, numbing, avoidant, and hyperarousal symptoms that generally parallels the symptom profile of PTSD seen in adults. As with adults, child and adolescent PTSD symptoms are positively correlated with the degree (intensity, duration, and life threat) of trauma exposure (Foy, Madvig, Pynoos, and Camilleri, in press). Despite the consistency of the PTSD construct across age groups, several features unique to child and adolescent PTSD have been identified. For example, whereas school-age children and adolescents tend to exhibit more classic symptoms of PTSD, preschool children tend to reexperience trauma through behavioral or play reenactments (repetitive play marked by trauma-related themes). Reexperiencing symptoms may also appear in the form of nightmares and night terrors similar to those experienced by adults. However, although these dreams may initially be specific to the trauma, they may later transform into nonspecific themes of direct or symbolic threat (such as being chased by monsters). Dissociative flashbacks and psychogenic amnesia are less well-established in children, although dissociation is more likely in cases of sexual or physical abuse.

Although not established empirically, clinical observations suggest that childhood PTSD may differ from that in adults because traumatic events tend to disrupt advancement through critical developmental tasks and transitions. Thus, in order to understand the effects of traumatic events on children, the interaction of the trauma with the child's developmental level must be considered. In general, children may be more vulnerable to less extreme stressors than adults due to their limited coping resources. Additionally, strong correlations between child and parent PTSD symptoms suggest that the reactions of important attachment figures may act as a key mediator in children's distress reactions. Children also exhibit unique cognitive-perceptual distortions, as evidenced by the tendency to underestimate or overestimate the proximity, duration, or sequencing of the traumatic event in direct proportion to degree of life threat. Other forms of cognitive distortions include the introduction of premonitions or omens of the event and imagined plans of action into episodic recall (such as a child remembering that he comforted a dying girl whom he was not able to get near). Trauma-related interruption of psychosocial development may also result in regression to an earlier maturational state, loss of recently acquired developmental skills, or lack of progress in accomplishing important developmental tasks (Pynoos and Nader, 1993).

Assessment of PTSD in Children and Adolescents

The study of PTSD in children and adolescents has not focused on a single trauma type, so methodological consistency is lacking, especially with respect to assessment instruments. Many researchers have modified adult-focused instruments, such as the DIS, or have drawn directly from DSM-III-R criteria without reporting any reliability or validity data. Recently, PTSD modules have been developed in several child-focused structured or semistructured interviews, including the Diagnostic Interview for Children and Adolescents (Herjanic, Herjanic, Brown, and Wheatt, 1975), the Child and Adolescent Psychiatric Assessment (Angold and others, 1987), and the Diagnostic Interview Schedule for Children (Costello and others, 1984). Although these instruments are promising, psychometric data on PTSD modules are not yet available. Several PTSD-specific instruments have also been developed. The Children's PTSD Inventory (Saigh, 1989) is a seventeen-item semistructured interview based on DSM-III-R criteria. It obtained a true positive rate of 84 percent in field trials. The Child Post-Traumatic Stress Reaction Index (RI) (Pynoos and others, 1993) is a twenty-item instrument, based on DSM-III and DSM-III-R criteria, that can be administered as a self-report measure or an interview. The RI has reasonably good internal consistency and inter-rater reliability, with mounting evidence of concurrent validity (Finch and Daugherty, 1993). As mentioned earlier, the Los Angeles Symptom Checklist (LASC) (Leskin and Foy, 1993) is a forty-three-item self-report measure that includes an adolescent version. The instrument has high internal consistency and test-retest reliability and satisfactory concurrent validity.

Parent and teacher rating scales have also been used to assess overall distress levels. Although PTSD is highly correlated with a variety of internalizing and externalizing behaviors and emotional distress indicators, these instruments have not consistently differentiated PTSD cases from other forms of childhood psychopathology. Thus, although they may be used as general screening measures, they should not be used to diagnose PTSD (Finch and Daugherty, 1993).

Conclusion

Although symptoms of PTSD are almost universal immediately after severe trauma exposure, rates tend to decline during the first three months post-trauma and then stabilize. For many survivors, avoidance of traumatic cues, both external as well as physiological or cognitive, becomes a guiding principle for maintaining psychological safety. The primary focus of assessment and treatment is the nature of the trauma and survivor reactions during and after the traumatic event. In children and adolescents, consideration of developmental issues is important for understanding symptom manifestations as well as potential developmental disruptions.

References

American Psychiatric Association. *Diagnostic and Statistical Manual of Mental Disorders.* (3rd ed.) Washington, D.C.: American Psychiatric Association, 1980.

Angold, A., Cox, A., Prendergast, M., Rutter, M., and Simonoff, E. *The Child and Adolescent Psychiatric Assessment (CAPA)*. Unpublished manuscript, 1987.

Astin, M. C., Ogland-Hand, S. M., Coleman, E. M., and Foy, D. W. "Post-Traumatic Stress Disorder and Childhood Abuse in Battered Women: Comparisons with Maritally Distressed Controls." *Journal of Consulting and Clinical Psychology*, in press.

Blake, D. D., Weathers, F. W., Nagy, L. M., Kaloupek, D. G., Klauminzer, G., Charney, D. S., and Keane, T. M. *Clinician-Administered PTSD Scale Form 1 (CAPS-1): Current and Lifetime Diagnosis Version*. Boston: National Center for PTSD, Behavioral Sciences Division, 1990.

Briere, J., and Runtz, M. "Post Sexual Abuse Trauma: Data and Implications for Clinical Practice." *Journal of Interpersonal Violence*, 1987, *2*, 367–379.

Briere, J., and Zaidi, L. Y. "Sexual Abuse Histories and Sequelae in Female Psychiatric Emergency Room Patients." *American Journal of Psychiatry*, 1989, *146*, 1602–1606.

Costello, A. J., Edelbrock, L. A., Dulcan, M. K., Kalas, R., and Klaric, S. H. *Report on the NIMH Diagnostic Interview Schedule for Children (DISC)*. Washington, D.C.: National Institute for Mental Health, 1984.

Creamer, M., Burgess, P., and Pattison, P. "Reaction to Trauma: A Cognitive-Processing Model." *Journal of Abnormal Psychology*, 1992, *101*, 452–459.

Finch, A. J., and Daugherty, T. K. "Issues in the Assessment of Posttraumatic Stress Disorder in Children." In C. F. Saylor (ed.), *Children and Disasters*. New York: Plenum Press, 1993.

Finkelhor, D., Hotaling, G., Lewis, I. A., and Smith, C. "Sexual Abuse in a National Survey of Adult Men and Women: Prevalence, Characteristics, and Risk Factors." *Child Abuse and Neglect*, 1990, *14*, 19–28.

Foy, D. W., Madvig, B. T., Pynoos, R. S., and Camilleri, A. "Etiologic Factors in the Development of Posttraumatic Stress Disorder in Children and Adolescents." *Journal of School Psychology*, in press.

Foy, D. W., Resnick, H. S., Sipprelle, R. C., and Carroll, E. M. "Premilitary, Military, and Postmilitary Factors in the Development of Combat-Related Posttraumatic Stress Disorder." *The Behavior Therapist*, 1987, *10*, 3–9.

Foy, D. W., Sipprelle, R. C., Rueger, D. B., and Carroll, E. M. "Etiology of Posttraumatic Stress Disorder in Vietnam Veterans: Analysis of Premilitary, Military, and Combat Exposure Influences." *Journal of Consulting and Clinical Psychology*, 1984, *52*, 79–87.

Helzer, J. E., Robins, L. N., and McEnvoy, L. "Post-Traumatic Stress Disorder in the General Population: Findings of the Epidemiological Catchment Area Survey." *New England Journal of Medicine*, 1987, *317*, 1630–1634.

Herjanic, B., Herjanic, M., Brown, F., and Wheatt, T. "Are Children Reliable Reporters?" *Journal of Abnormal Child Psychology*, 1975, *3*, 41–48.

Horowitz, M. J. *Stress Response Syndromes*. North Vale, N.J.: Jason Aronson, 1986.

Horowitz, M. J., Wilner, N., and Alvarez, W. "Impact of Event Scale: A Measure of Subjective Distress." *Psychosomatic Medicine*, 1979, *41*, 209–218.

Houskamp, B. M., and Foy, D. W. "The Assessment of Posttraumatic Stress Disorder in Battered Women." *Journal of Interpersonal Violence*, 1991, *6*, 367–375.

Janoff-Bulman, R. *Shattered Assumptions*. New York: Free Press, 1992.

Jordan, K. B. "Lifetime and Current Prevalence of Specific Psychiatric Disorders Among Vietnam Veterans and Controls." *Archives of General Psychiatry*, 1991, *48*, 207–215.

Kilpatrick, D. G., and Resnick, H. S. "Posttraumatic Stress Disorder Associated with Exposure to Criminal Victimization in Clinical and Community Populations." In J.R.T. Davidson and E. B. Foa (eds.), *Posttraumatic Stress Disorder: DSM-IV and Beyond*. Washington, D.C.: American Psychiatric Press, 1993.

Kilpatrick, D. G., Saunders, B. E., Veronen, L. J., Best, C. L., and Von, J. M. "Criminal Victimization: Lifetime Prevalence Reporting to Police, and Psychological Impact." *Crime and Delinquency*, 1987, *33*, 479–489.

Koverola, C., and Foy, D. "Posttraumatic Stress Disorder Symptomatology in Sexually Abused Children: Implications for Legal Proceedings." *Journal of Child Sexual Abuse,* 1993, *2,* 119–128.

Kulka, R. A., Schlenger, W. E., Fairbank, J. A., Hough, R. L., Jordan, B. K., Marmar, C. R., and Weiss, D. S. *Trauma and the Vietnam War Generation.* New York: Brunner/Mazel, 1990.

Leskin, G. R., and Foy, D. W. *Psychometric Properties of the Los Angeles Symptom Checklist.* Paper presented at the International Society for Traumatic Stress Studies, San Antonio, Tex., Nov. 1993.

McLeer, A. V., Deblinger, E., Atkins, M. S., Foa, E. B., and Ralphe, D. L. "Post-Traumatic Stress Disorder in Sexually Abused Children." *Journal of the American Academy of Child and Adolescent Psychiatry,* 1988, *27,* 650–654.

Olasov Rothbaum, B., and Foa, E. B. "Subtypes of Posttraumatic Stress Disorder and Duration of Symptoms." In J.R.T. Davidson and E. B. Foa (eds.), *Posttraumatic Stress Disorder: DSM-IV and Beyond.* Washington, D.C.: American Psychiatric Press, 1993.

Pitman, R. K. "Biological Findings in Posttraumatic Stress Disorder: Implications for DSM-IV Classification." In J.R.T. Davidson and E. B. Foa (eds.), *Posttraumatic Stress Disorder: DSM-IV and Beyond.* Washington, D.C.: American Psychiatric Press, 1993.

Pynoos, R. S., Goenjian, A., Tashjian, M., Karakashian, M., Manjikian, R., Manoukian, G., Steinberg, A. M., and Fairbanks, L. "Post-Traumatic Stress Reactions in Children After the 1988 Armenian Earthquake." *British Journal of Psychiatry,* 1993, *163,* 239–247.

Pynoos, R. S., and Nader, K. "Issues in the Treatment of Posttraumatic Stress in Children and Adolescents." In J. P. Wilson and B. Raphael (eds.), *International Handbook of Traumatic Stress Syndromes.* New York: Plenum, 1993.

Rausch, K., and Knutson, J. F. "The Self-Report of Personal Punitive Experiences and Those of Siblings." *Child Abuse and Neglect,* 1991, *15,* 29–36.

Resick, P. A., and Schnicke, M. K. "Cognitive Processing Therapy for Sexual Assault Victims." *Journal of Consulting and Clinical Psychology,* 1992, *60,* 748–756.

Richters, J. R., and Martinez, P. "The NIMH Community Violence Project: Children as Victims and Witnesses to Violence." *Journal of Psychiatry,* 1993, *56,* 7–21.

Rowan, A. B., Foy, D. W., Rodriguez, N., and Ryan, S. "Posttraumatic Stress Disorder in Adults Sexually Abused as Children." *Child Abuse and Neglect,* 1994, *18,* 51–61.

Saigh, P. A. "The Development and Validation of the Children's PTSD Inventory." *International Journal of Special Education,* 1989, *4,* 75–84.

Solomon, A., and Mikulincer, M. "Psychological Sequelae of War: A 2-Year Follow-Up Study of Israeli Combat Stress Reaction Casualties." *Journal of Nervous and Mental Disease,* 1988, *176,* 264–269.

Spitzer, R. L., Williams, J. B., Gibbon, M., and First, M. B. *Structured Clinical Interview for DSM-III-R-Patient Edition (SCID-P).* New York: Biometrics Research Department, New York State Psychiatric Institute, 1989.

Straus, M. A. "Measuring Intrafamily Conflict and Violence: The Conflict Tactic (CT) Scales." *Journal of Marriage and the Family,* 1979, *41,* 75–87.

Straus, M. A., and Gelles, R. J. "Societal Change and Change in Family Violence from 1975 to 1985 as Revealed by Two National Surveys." *Journal of Marriage and the Family,* 1986, *48,* 465–479.

Weiss, D., Marmar, C. R., Metzler, T., and Ronfeldt, H. "Predicting Symptom Stress in Emergency Service Personnel." *Journal of Consulting and Clinical Psychology,* in press.

MILLIE C. ASTIN, Ph.D., is research project director at the Center for Trauma Recovery, University of Missouri-St. Louis.

CHRISTOPHER M. LAYNE, M.A., is a doctoral student in clinical psychology at University of California at Los Angeles.

ANGELA J. CAMILLERI, M.A., has recently completed her master's degree in psychology at Pepperdine University.

DAVID W. FOY, Ph.D., is professor of psychology at the Graduate School of Education and Psychology, Pepperdine University, and part-time staff psychologist at the West Los Angeles Veterans Administration Medical Center, Brentwood Division.

PART TWO

Treatment

Principles of optimal treatment for sexual abuse victims are presented, including separation of psychotherapy from forensic investigation, the need for a child-focused orientation, and time-specific involvement of different treatment modalities.

Treating Child Victims of Sexual Abuse

Cheryl B. Lanktree

This chapter describes treatment for sexually abused children and nonoffending family members. The focus is on the child victim's recovery from abuse-related trauma and on his or her longer-term psychological adjustment, as well as on strengthening the functioning of the supportive family system.

Treatment of Sexually Abused Children: The Stuart House Model

The interventions described are provided by Stuart House, a Santa Monica, California treatment center based on the multidisciplinary child advocacy model (Lind, 1991; Reece, 1992). Investigative and treatment services are provided separately, by separate personnel, to sexually abused children in a coordinated, collaborative manner at one site. Joint investigative interviews are conducted by specialized professionals including law enforcement officers, deputy district attorneys, and child protective services workers, but never child therapists. Specialized, evidentiary medical examinations are also available. The child is then typically referred for clinical services, including evaluation and treatment.

Suspected victims of sexual abuse aged two to eighteen years receive the services necessary to facilitate criminal prosecution, child protection, and emotional recovery. The same professionals involved in the investigation continue with the child and the family when further legal or protective services are indicated, including during any court procedures. The same therapist completes the

I wish to thank Gail Abarbanel, director of the Rape Treatment Center, Santa Monica Hospital Medical Center, for her leadership and guidance of Stuart House and for her support of my research endeavors.

initial phone intake and the initial diagnostic evaluation and provides treatment if treatment is recommended.

Because this model is victim-oriented and especially concerned with creating a safe, child-oriented environment, no alleged perpetrators receive treatment at Stuart House. Family therapy involving the alleged or admitted perpetrator may include the child's therapist at another site once the perpetrator has received sufficient treatment. The child's emotional needs are the priority—a focus that may not have been the case before. When more than one child in the family has been sexually abused or traumatized by the disclosure, each child is assigned his or her own therapist. This model does not allow the therapist to conduct investigations, just as the investigators do not do therapy.

In some communities, the roles of investigator and therapist become merged due to limited resources or overlapping responsibilities. This is likely to be confusing to the child and can undermine the therapeutic relationship, particularly if the therapist is primarily concerned with determining "the truth" about allegations or with obtaining further abuse disclosures. New substantive disclosures of abuse must be reported, but the emphasis of work in therapy is on the healing process.

Effectiveness of the Stuart House Treatment Model

In these times of fiscal restraint and depletion of treatment resources, it is critical that treatment programs be evaluated regarding their effectiveness in resolving symptomatology. A common belief is that because children are thought to be resilient, longer-term therapy is rarely necessary. A four-year study of the effectiveness of Stuart House treatment (Lanktree and Briere, 1994), however, has shown that not only do many sexually traumatized children require more than crisis intervention or short-term treatment, but the recovery process may involve differential rates of resolution for specific symptoms of trauma.

This study examined treatment outcome in 105 male and female sexually abused children, aged eight to fifteen years, and found that their scores on five subscales of the Trauma Symptom Checklist for Children (TSCC) (Briere, in press)—depression, anxiety, posttraumatic stress, dissociation, and anger—decreased significantly after three months of therapy and continued to decrease significantly at later points in treatment. However, sexual concerns (such as sexualized behaviors and sexual preoccupations) began to decrease significantly only after six months of treatment.

These data indicate that treatment for sexually abused children can be effective, and that the specific treatment technology used by Stuart House staff is worthy of more detailed description. The following sections outline this treatment approach in terms of general treatment principles.

First Stage: Clinical Evaluation

Although the evaluation process continues throughout treatment, an initial clinical evaluation occurs during the first two or three sessions, with separate sessions for the child client and available primary caretakers. In addition, parent-child sessions may be required when a preschool age child is unwilling to separate from his or her parent or when it is necessary to assess the parent-child relationship. The child and nonoffending caretakers are informed of the parameters of confidentiality: information from sessions is shared only when a child is at risk of being harmed by another or is at risk for self-harm, child abuse is suspected, or a serious threat is being made to harm someone else.

The following areas are usually considered necessary for a complete evaluation.

Presenting problem and associated symptoms. The presenting problem includes information from the initial referral, such as any disclosure or suspicion of sexual abuse and general information regarding the child's emotional and behavioral functioning. It is important to determine whether the child or adolescent is in crisis, especially in terms of possible suicidality.

Developmental history. All prenatal information, circumstances of conception (planned or unplanned pregnancy), nature of delivery, and developmental milestones should be obtained. This information (or lack thereof) can be very revealing of the early parent-child relationship. If there was an early separation, such as when parents emigrate without their children to the United States, there may be a higher risk of physical abuse by a parent (Lynch, 1975). Clinical experience also suggests that impaired parent-child attachment may follow from early separation, a dynamic that places the child at greater vulnerability to being sexually abused by said parent. An impaired parent-child relationship can also compromise protection by a nonoffending caretaker. Furthermore, early developmental disabilities can place the child at greater risk for abuse and make him or her more vulnerable to the later psychological effects of abuse.

Family history. Information should be gathered regarding the families of origin for both parents of the child victim, circumstances of the parents' current (and any major previous) relationships, the child's birth order and siblings' ages, serious illnesses and deaths of family members, and relationships between family members. A family genogram can be very informative regarding family background and the context of the child's and family's responses to the sexual abuse.

Sexual abuse and other maltreatment. It is important that all available details concerning the reported sexual abuse be described in the child's or informant's own words. Because the evaluation is part of the record that can later be subpoenaed, the clinician must avoid any unnecessarily interpretive statements.

The circumstances of the abuse, responses of family members (including extended family members), emotional and behavioral reactions of the child, and any associated safety concerns (such as family pressure on child to recant or to visit with alleged perpetrator) should be included. In addition, any history of previous abuse (sexual, physical, or emotional) of the child victim and other family members should be described.

Mental status and social history of the child client. The child should be thoroughly assessed regarding symptomatology (observed and by history), including depression and trauma-related symptoms (such as dissociation, posttraumatic stress, fear, and anxiety), as well as current coping strategies. Suicidal ideation is particularly prevalent in child and adolescent sexual abuse victims (Lanktree, Briere, and Zaidi, 1991; Briere and Runtz, 1986). If suicidality is an issue, contracts should be made or other preventive measures enacted as necessary (for example, the child or caretakers agree to contact the therapist if the child feels suicidal and the therapist agrees to contact the child between sessions in times of crisis). The child's functioning with peers and at school should be explored in relation to the abuse as well as before the abuse.

Clinical formulations and development of the treatment plan. Long-standing family issues or parental psychopathology may necessitate that other treatment modalities, such as individual therapy for a parent, be combined with abuse-focused treatment for the child. The child client may be especially fearful of abuse-related material due to the extraordinary conflict between his or her parents. In such a situation, if the child is not in immediate danger and has not disclosed any sexual abuse, the family may have to be referred elsewhere to a treatment setting that can address the family issues, increase the level of support for the child, and eventually address possible sexual abuse. A child who is experiencing a lack of support at home but who is asked, nevertheless, to deal with alleged sexual abuse may experience such conflicting pressures that his or her emotional well-being is substantially undermined.

Once the treatment plan (including target problems, treatment modalities, and goals) is designed, it should be evaluated regularly through weekly supervision and consultation, periodic review of the treatment record, and quality assurance studies. Without ongoing monitoring, treatment can become diffuse and unfocused, particularly with less-experienced clinicians. Measures evaluating symptoms, such as the TSCC and the Child Behavior Checklist (Achenbach and Edelbrock, 1979), administered at regular intervals, can also provide direction for treatment interventions.

Therapy Approaches

Abuse-focused therapy incorporates such diverse approaches as play therapy, cognitive behavioral treatment, and psychodynamic therapy. Interventions are adjusted according to the child or adolescent's developmental level. Underlying theoretical principles are derived from social learning theory, developmental psychology, systems theory, attachment theory, and object relations theory. Major principles of abuse-focused therapy include the following:

Reported or suspected sexual abuse and associated symptoms, as determined by ongoing evaluation, provide the focus for treatment.

Child victims and traumatized siblings in treatment are the primary clients. The therapeutic environment is child-oriented and provides advocacy for children in other relevant systems such as criminal or family court.

The therapist monitors and maintains clear, consistent boundaries between treatment and the investigation, focusing on the emotional healing of the child and the family.

The usual rules of therapist-client privilege and confidentiality are vigilantly observed to optimize a sense of safety and protection. Because legal issues often arise in abuse cases, the therapist is aware of potential repercussions associated with any release of information and explains these issues to the parent or holder of the privilege.

Multiple therapeutic modalities are typically combined with individual therapy. Most children participate in some form of family therapy and many attend group therapy. Most primary caregivers are encouraged to participate in collateral therapy.

Preparation of the Therapist. Any therapist working in the highly specialized field of abuse-focused therapy must first achieve a solid grounding in general psychotherapy skills. In addition, the therapist experienced in treating sexual abuse trauma with adults must have specialized training in child treatment before working with child sexual abuse victims.

One of the major challenges to therapists treating children is the variability in behavior and emotional issues associated with different developmental stages. The child therapist must be knowledgeable in developmental psychology and should be current with the literature on the impacts of abuse-related trauma on psychological development. He or she must be prepared to address these issues with sensitivity to cultural differences and with awareness of environmental stressors such as poverty and living in a violent neighborhood.

Therapeutic Modalities. It is paramount that the child experience safety, support, and encouragement as she or he explores traumatic experiences with the therapist. Many child abuse programs provide only group therapy to children. This approach may be incomplete, however, because most children need to (at least initially) explore upsetting material in a one-to-one, trusting relationship with a therapist. Just as most clinicians would not immediately place an adult abuse survivor in a treatment group without adequate individual treatment, the same is true for most child victims. Although group therapy is an important adjunctive form of treatment for many children and adolescents, it is usually best initiated after sufficient individual therapy has transpired.

Stage Approach to Individual Therapy

In general, individual therapy typically follows certain stages as the child becomes more accustomed to the therapeutic relationship. The stages described here are not inevitable and can overlap. Many children and adolescents will return to earlier stages as they begin to explore more threatening material or more intense abuse-related feelings.

The initial stage of therapeutic engagement begins during the evaluation stage and primarily involves rapport-building. This process is concomitant with further assessment of the child's mental status, behavioral symptoms, the nature of possible sexual abuse (and other) maltreatment, and the child's response to treatment.

The next stage of therapy involves greater involvement in therapeutic games and other activities that facilitate the development of communication skills and expression of feelings. As the child client becomes more comfortable with the therapist, he or she will explore issues and feelings directly related to his or her sense of self and identity, including self-perceptions, self-esteem, and self-efficacy. Because a stable sense of self and inner resources may be required before in-depth work on traumatic events and feelings can be initiated, play therapy activities that focus on the development and reinforcement of self and healthy coping strategies are an important component throughout therapy. As therapy continues, additional aspects of distress or dysfunction are addressed. As indicated by research described earlier (Lanktree and Briere, 1994), these include dysphoria (depression, anxiety, and anger), posttraumatic stress (including dissociation), and sexual difficulties.

In any given session, a client may progress from initial rapport-building to expressive and communication work (for example, moving from playing Candyland to drawing pictures depicting feelings) to identity and self work (such as a collage of what they like and who they are) to more directly abuse-focused material (such as play with dolls reenacting abuse incidents). Over time, the typical traumatized child will gradually approach increasingly more difficult (more trauma-related) material over successive sessions.

A common dilemma in abuse-focused therapy is whether to push abuse work when a child is avoidant. Because children and adolescents typically do not seek therapy themselves, avoidance and ambivalence regarding therapy are common. A skilled therapist can gradually desensitize a traumatized child to the sharing of anxiety-arousing material with gentle, inviting comments such as "I know that it is very difficult to come here and talk" or "You are a very brave boy for coming here to talk about your feelings." If a child has previously disclosed, the therapist may be more direct with comments such as "I know that you've talked to [the investigative interviewers]. Can you try to talk about it, or maybe show me [enact with dolls, stuffed animals, or sand tray] what happened?" The child may initiate more play focused on trauma as he or she experiences safety and support within the therapeutic relationship.

The therapist might suggest possible activities to further this work, such as playing a board game that incorporates general abuse-related questions, reading a story about a child or animal who was abused, or enacting feelings toward the perpetrator or about the abuse. This process is analogous to the systematic desensitization of a phobia in that a child is encouraged and supported to approach increasingly more sensitive, anxiety-arousing material. He or she can return to more neutral or soothing activities and discussion when the anxiety becomes overwhelming. If the client continues to be extremely avoidant and evidences high anxiety, the clinician should investigate possible causes for this avoidance and work to increase the child's sense of safety.

Especially for clients who have posttraumatic and dissociative symptoms, it is important that the therapist work to alleviate the anxiety and dysphoria that may be preventing the child from dealing with his or her abuse. As the child client gains greater skill in expressing feelings verbally and symbolically through play, he or she can become more confident in his or her sense of self and internal resources, more trusting of the therapist, and more able to confront the especially difficult aspects of the abuse. The therapist may also have to address the factors or circumstances contributing to the dissociation and posttraumatic stress, such as ongoing exposure to an abusive parent.

Sexual issues, such as sexual acting-out and sexual preoccupations, can be addressed in individual therapy by exploring the underlying feelings and by developing alternative coping strategies that the child can use when feeling anxious or fearful. Group therapy also can be particularly effective. Treatment interventions specifically designed to alleviate sexual symptoms (Friedrich, 1990; Gil and Johnson, 1993) also may be used.

Collateral Treatment Services: Working with Primary Caretakers

Although the treatment model described here focuses on providing therapy for the primary victim, treatment is also provided to significant nonoffending caretakers, as well as siblings who manifest symptoms of trauma.

As research and clinical practice have demonstrated (Conte and Berliner, 1988), the extent of support provided by significant caretakers is one of the most important factors in the recovery of child sexual abuse victims. In order to assist caretakers in their own recovery from their child's victimization (as well as, in some cases, their own victimization), treatment must take into account the caretaker's own level of functioning. Several common caretaker presentations are described below, along with their prognoses.

Caretakers who have good attachment relationships with their child, are supportive caretakers, and are able to explore their own reactions to their child's abuse while making their child's needs the priority. Collateral therapy may be short-term unless other traumatic material surfaces for the child or parent, or other crises arise such as a criminal trial. The prognosis is very good for the child and the parent with consistent participation in treatment of child and family.

Caretakers who have at least a fair attachment to their child and had good parenting skills before their child's victimization, but have become emotionally overwhelmed by their own past victimization memories, which are restimulated by the child's abuse. The prognosis is good if the caretaker engages in his or her own treatment, is provided with collateral services (such as individual sessions or a parents' group), and is supportive of his or her child's treatment (attends consistently and does not undermine the therapist's interventions).

Caretakers who have difficult (anxious or avoidant) attachments, history of extensive trauma, or possibly early separation from child, but who respond supportively toward the child at the time of disclosure of sexual abuse. This may be a caretaker who recently engaged in his or her own therapy before the child's disclosure of abuse, or a parent who is superficially supportive of their child but minimizes the impact of the abuse on their child. The prognosis is often good with consistent participation of the child in individual therapy and the caretaker in collateral and individual therapy. Nonoffending caretakers in this group may press for reunification with the perpetrator, but can be amenable to increasing their support of the child victim through therapeutic interventions.

Caretakers who have a difficult attachment relationship with the child and continue to demonstrate an inability to support and care for the child following disclosure (may even be more avoidant and rejecting after abuse is disclosed). Although in most cases removal of the child from the nonoffending caretaker is not recommended, this may be necessary when the caretaker continues to be emotionally abusive with the child victim, fails to protect the child from further abuse, and is not amenable to change. This parent may also pressure the child to recant the abuse and pursue reunification with the perpetrator despite the potential negative impact on the child. The prognosis may be fair to good for the child if he or she is old enough to benefit from therapy even without support from the nonoffending parent. Otherwise, this caretaker presentation is often associated with treatment failure.

Collateral sessions often provide an opportunity for the therapist to form relationships with the primary caregivers who are responsible for bringing child clients to treatment, to intervene to improve parenting skills, to educate parents regarding child sexual abuse, to support caregivers through their reactions to their child's abuse, and to implement change in the family system. Collateral treatment is essential for successful treatment of most younger child victims. Older adolescents who are not being emotionally supported by caretakers may not benefit from the involvement of these caretakers in their treatment.

Family Therapy Approaches

Before engaging in family therapy with families where sexual abuse has occurred, the therapist should have extensive training and experience in treating families who have general communication and relationship problems. Knowledge regarding the principles of systems functioning, general family therapy interventions, the art of engaging family members and establishing alliances, and effective confrontation of dysfunctional behaviors to implement change is essential.

A thorough assessment of family functioning before and after disclosure should also precede family therapy. Family therapy is appropriate when nonoffending caretakers demonstrate at least some empathy for their children and are amenable to change. The family should also be open to developing better boundaries and more appropriate roles and, especially, acknowledging the responsibility for the victimization as residing with the perpetrator and not the victim. Family therapy is most effective when the victim can describe the abuse incidents to family members in the therapy session, express his or her feelings associated with the abuse, and receive support from family members.

Family therapy is not appropriate when there is a possibility of violence or abuse occurring in response to such sessions. For example, if a parent becomes verbally abusive toward a child following a family therapy session wherein the child has confronted the parent, it is important for the therapist to resume individual therapy sessions to explore these issues. When a nonoffending parent is overwhelmed by his or her own reactions and cannot be emotionally supportive of his or her child, no family therapy sessions should be conducted until the parent has had sufficient individual therapy. Family therapy sessions that include an offending family member (someone who has sexually abused the child) should not occur until that individual has taken responsibility for the abuse, is in successful individual therapy, and is amenable to continued change.

Beyond these constraints, family therapy should be considered whenever possible. Treatment should include all family members who interact with the child because that system affects the child on a daily basis. If other members are not motivated to become more supportive of the child victim, it may be necessary to conduct family therapy sessions with only the nonoffending parent and child. Therapists must be flexible and assess the readiness of other family members to participate in sessions on an ongoing basis.

The therapist must form alliances with all available family members without overlooking the fact that crimes have been committed against the child. If the perpetrator eventually participates, it may be more appropriate for a clinician other than the child victim's or the perpetrator's therapist to conduct the family therapy sessions, although this clinician may collaborate with the other therapists involved. Unfortunately, family therapists without training in sexual abuse can overcontextualize the abuse and prematurely direct the family toward reunification. It should be reiterated, however, that at all times the emotional welfare and safety of the child who has been victimized—as well as the other children in the family—is the paramount concern.

Clear guidelines regarding the incest perpetrator's role in the family, timing of visits, limits on the perpetrator's behavior during visits, and arrangements for monitoring or supervision should be established. He or she should never return to a position of authority and power over the children in the family. Behavioral programs may also be helpful to establish more positive relationships between family members; for example, nonoffending parents can learn to reward the child's completion of household tasks or to increase the appropriate expression of affection.

Improved communication of feelings without use of coercion or verbal abuse is modeled and developed in family sessions. Greater problem-solving skills, expansion of self-efficacy skills, and development of support systems outside the family are typical goals for all family members. In addition, when a family has enforced rigid sex roles, it is helpful to expand the choices for all family members (for example, increasing the assertiveness of a traditional mother) while also being sensitive to cultural factors.

Families with long-standing issues may require a longer course of family therapy (one or two years or more) to establish healthier functioning and to reduce the risk of further victimization. Marital therapy may also be required before family therapy can proceed any further.

Interventions that are more effective tend to be based on structural family therapy (Minuchin and Fishman, 1981; Minuchin, 1984) and strategic family therapy (Haley, 1987; Papp, 1983), approaches that are oriented toward changing roles and family interactions. At times of crisis, family members may regress to more destructive patterns with each other. The therapist may need to increase the level of support during such times, with more frequent family sessions and with support outside family therapy (such as accompanying the family to court or providing advocacy and referrals for child care or financial assistance).

Group Therapy: Models of Treatment Groups

As noted earlier, group therapy is typically begun later in treatment for the child or adolescent victim. This is often not true for caretakers, who can benefit more immediately from the support and information provided in group sessions. In general, such groups can provide peer support, information about child sexual abuse, strategies for coping, prevention and safety skills, and opportunities to describe details of the abuse that can reduce trauma-related symptoms.

Group treatment can advance the gains derived from individual sessions, often in dramatic and enduring ways. Members often disclose more details of the abuse and associated trauma when encouraged by their peers' courage and support. When a child or parent has just begun individual treatment or is continuing to work on major trust issues, group therapy may be offered in combination with some individual sessions.

Effective group treatment for sexual abuse victims is structured and time-limited with same-sex individuals who are similar in age (such as nine to eleven years or thirteen to fifteen years) and in type of sexual abuse history (extrafamilial or intrafamilial abuse). It is usually advisable that two co-therapists conduct groups of six to eight members.

Groups for mothers, many of whom have victimization histories themselves, often follow a two-stage model: the first phase (approximately eight to twelve weeks) focuses on support, parent education, sexual abuse information, family dynamics, coping strategies, sex roles and relationships, and an initial exploration of participants' own victimization histories. For caretakers who acknowledge an abuse history and are amenable to further work, a second group—generally with the same members—focuses in greater depth on issues of sexuality, relationships and choices of partners, abuse histories and associated trauma, and exploration of self and identity issues apart from the parent role. Caretaker groups, including primary caregivers such as parents, grandparents, and aunts may be conducted in conjunction with the younger (latency and preadolescent) groups as recommended by Mandell and colleagues (1989).

Conclusion

This chapter has described some of the interventions and approaches used to treat sexually abused children and their families. The ideal circumstances for treatment appear to involve a separation of treatment from the investigation process. In this way, the therapist, while still maintaining an advocacy role, can focus more on the healing process of the child and family. Supervision and peer support are essential for all therapists, no matter how seasoned, to balance the often competing agendas of professionalism and personal investment. Different treatment modalities are invoked at different points in therapy, and attention is paid not only to the child victim but also to his or her nonoffending caretakers and other family members.

References

Achenbach, T. M., and Edelbrock, C. S. "The Child Behavior Profile: II. Boys Aged 12–16 and Girls Aged 6–11 and 12–16." *Journal of Consulting and Clinical Psychology*, 1979, 47, 223–233.

Briere, J. *Child Abuse Trauma: Theory and Treatment of the Lasting Effects*. Newbury Park, Calif.: Sage, 1992.

Briere, J. *Professional Manual for the Trauma Symptom Checklist for Children (TSCC)*. Odessa, Fla.: Psychological Assessment Resources, in press.

Briere, J., and Runtz, M. "Suicidal Thoughts and Behaviors in Former Sexual Abuse Victims." *Canadian Journal of Behavioural Science*, 1986, 18, 413–423.

Conte, J. R., and Berliner, L. "The Impact of Sexual Abuse on Children: Empirical Findings." In L.E.A. Walker (ed.), *Handbook on Sexual Abuse of Children*. New York: Springer, 1988.

Friedrich, W. N. *Psychotherapy of Sexually Abused Children and Their Families*. New York: W. W. Norton, 1990.

Gil, E., and Johnson, T. C. *Sexualized Children: Assessment and Treatment of Sexualized Children and Children Who Molest*. Rockville, Md.: Launch Press, 1993.

Haley, J. *Problem-Solving Therapy*. (2nd ed.) San Francisco: Jossey-Bass, 1987.

Lanktree, C. B., and Briere, J. *Outcome of Therapy for Sexually Abused Children: A Longitudinal Study.* Unpublished manuscript, 1994.

Lanktree, C. B., Briere, J., and Zaidi, L. Y. "Incidence and Impacts of Sexual Abuse in a Child Outpatient Sample: The Role of Direct Inquiry." *Child Abuse and Neglect,* 1991, *15,* 447–453.

Lind, J. "Children's Advocacy Centers." *The Advisor,* 1991, *4,* 12.

Lynch, M. "Ill Health and Child Abuse." *Lancet,* Aug. 16, 1975.

Mandell, J. G., Damon, L., Castaldo, P. C., Tauber, E. S., Monise, L., and Larsen, N. F. *Group Treatment for Sexually Abused Children.* New York: Guilford Press, 1989.

Minuchin, S. *Family Kaleidoscope.* Cambridge, Mass.: Harvard University Press, 1984.

Minuchin, S., and Fishman, H. C. *Family Therapy Techniques.* Cambridge, Mass.: Harvard University Press, 1981.

Papp, P. *The Process of Change.* New York: Guilford Press, 1983.

Reece, R. M. "Interdisciplinary Teams: Do They Help Victims of Child Abuse?" *The Advisor,* 1992, *5,* 15.

CHERYL B. LANKTREE, Ph.D., is clinical director of Stuart House, Santa Monica Hospital Medical Center, and assistant clinical professor, Department of Psychiatry, University of California at Los Angeles.

Literature regarding the aftermath of rape, the process of recovery from rape, and treatment is reviewed. Suggestions for conceptualizing a rape experience within the broader context of women's lives are given and specific intervention techniques are also reviewed.

Treatment of Adult Victims of Rape

Barbara J. Gilbert

Rape and sexual assault in adulthood affect the lives of as many as 44 percent of women (Russell, 1984). Although 20–25 percent of untreated sexual assault survivors report being relatively symptom-free one year post-assault (Kilpatrick, Resick, and Veronen, 1981), many report negative effects for a year or more (Burgess and Holmstrom, 1974; Calhoun, Atkeson, and Resick, 1982; Notman and Nadelson, 1976). Burgess and Holmstrom (1979) described a seventy-two-year-old woman who was raped in her twenties and avoided men and sexual behavior throughout her life. Time does not heal all wounds. If victims are to receive adequate assistance in recovering from rape, therapists must educate themselves about the aftermath of rape and appropriate, complete treatments for full recovery.

Although men, too, are raped in our culture, the present chapter focuses on sexual assaults against women. As more research and clinical practice take place in the area of male sexual victimization, it is hoped that chapters similar to the present one will be made available for those who treat this largely overlooked problem.

Aftermath of Sexual Assault

The damage of sexual assault can be extensive, involving the victim's physical, emotional, cognitive, relational, sexual, and spiritual satisfaction or functioning. The immediate and later reactions to rape are distinctly different. The immediate aftermath (days or weeks following the assault) is characterized by general stress response symptoms, whereas the longer-term reaction (lasting from months to years) is characterized by specifically rape-related symptoms (Burgess and Holmstrom, 1985).

Immediately after a sexual assault, physical symptoms arise that are similar to symptoms occurring after any extreme stress event, including nausea, headache, gastrointestinal problems, sleep and appetite disturbances, and nightmares. In addition, venereal disease and pregnancy may occur. The victim may have lacerations, abrasions, soreness, and bruising from tissue damage during the assault.

Victims experience fear or terror, anxiety, confusion, emotional numbness, restlessness, and anger in the immediate aftermath of sexual assault (Burgess and Holmstrom, 1974; Kilpatrick, Veronen, and Resick, 1979). Elevations on measures of depression, fear, anxiety, and social maladjustment are seen in all empirical studies (Anderson and Frank, 1991).

Aftereffects and the Context of Women's Lives

Clinical experience and sexual assault literature suggest that the context of a woman's life before the rape moderates its impact. I draw on four contextual elements for understanding the effects of violence on women's lives. These include relatedness as central to many women's gender identities (Gilligan, 1982), concern with control and security arising from economic dependence and oppression (Schwendinger and Schwendinger, 1983), indirectness as a strategy encouraged and adopted by many in the face of economic dependence and oppression (Gilbert, 1994), and the extreme importance placed on woman-as-body in our society (Greenspan, 1983). To the extent that a woman was socialized in a traditional way, we might expect her to experience relatedness as central to her identity as a woman; to be concerned with issues of control and security; to often find herself in conflict between relatedness and control or security concerns; to develop an indirect style for expressing her feelings and seeking what she wants or needs; and to consider her appearance and her sexual, reproductive, or caretaking abilities as her most important assets in seeking security and relatedness (Gilbert, 1994). Cultures might vary in their emphasis on these elements (relatedness may be more important in one culture than another), their definition of an element (such as physical attractiveness), or in their manifestation of an element (perhaps specific ways of being indirect are culturally defined), but there are few major present-day cultures in which these components of women's socialization and experience are absent entirely. Individual women might escape from, rebel against, or be protected from these influences, but cultures as a whole still support them.

Given this context for the traditionally socialized woman, predictable consequences of rape may emerge in these four areas. Regarding relatedness, we would expect that the greater the bond between the victim and the rapist, the greater the damage to her sense of trust and her sense of self as a woman. She will probably feel very lost and ungrounded for a time. She might behave differently and more erratically and have difficulty making decisions and interacting with others.

The rape would significantly increase her concerns regarding control and security. If the rape unsettles a woman's sense of security a great deal (as it usually does), she might become demanding, withdrawn, dependent, and anxious, or engage in other versions of the fight, flight, or fright responses. Alternatively, she might give up seeking control, develop depression stemming from a sense of helplessness, and feel unable to perform tasks she previously performed masterfully.

Regarding the indirect style, to the extent that a woman has been socialized to express anger and wants indirectly, in the aftermath of rape she might develop depression stemming from repressed rage and she might develop somatic symptoms. She might also begin to act out her anger in hostile or self-destructive ways in order to express indirectly what she cannot express directly. In addition, she might use indirect strategies for reestablishing relatedness, security, and control— she might find herself seeking more social contact but not telling anyone about the rape; she might throw herself into work as a way to feel a sense of mastery at something, without addressing concerns regarding physical safety.

Finally, regarding woman-as-body, to the extent that a woman was socialized to believe that her body is her greatest asset, we would expect her to feel especially devalued following a rape, to feel that something was stolen from her, to feel dirty, impure, unworthy. She might feel less hopeful about her potential to gain relatedness and security if she expects to acquire these in marriage but feels she no longer is valuable enough to attract a marriage partner. In addition to these body-relatedness concerns, the rape also will probably raise concerns about body control. Even if she previously was socialized to use her body as a commodity or to accept others' treatment of her body as such, she may now feel that it is dangerous to do so. She may change her appearance (wear concealing clothes, gain weight, stop wearing makeup, or cut her hair). She may stop going out in public, in the conscious or unconscious hope of being less attractive or less visible as a body and therefore more in control of who might want her body. We would expect that the disruption in body-relatedness and body control would combine to make sexual activity confusing and fraught with anxiety. Apart from the effects of how society values women's bodies, sexual assault is one of the most intrusive, violating experiences possible. We would expect that the greater the violence of the intrusion, the greater her concern over bodily safety. She is also likely to feel specifically protective of her sexuality, which might add to sexual dissatisfaction or dysfunction or lead to a decision to be celibate. Alternatively, she may feel that her sexuality is no longer worth protecting and may allow or seek indiscriminate sex, or otherwise develop more permeable personal boundaries, which in turn could increase her vulnerability to sexual violence in the future. Research findings and other theories generally support the effects predicted from this contextual framework and are reviewed next.

Longer-Term Emotional Effects

Intermediate-term effects of sexual assault (occurring three months to one year post-assault) include depression and rape-specific anxiety rather than the more diffuse anxiety seen immediately after the assault (Anderson and Frank, 1991). Beyond one year post-assault, effects such as anger, diminished capacity to enjoy life, and hypervigilance to danger are common (Anderson and Frank, 1991; Ellis, Atkeson, and Calhoun, 1981). Burnam and others (1988) found that sexual assault victims were more likely than nonvictims to manifest major depression, drug abuse and dependence, phobia, panic disorder, and obsessive-compulsive disorder. Some of these disorders may increase vulnerability to future sexual assault.

Longer-Term Cognitive Effects

Clinicians, researchers, and victims themselves have noted longer-term negative effects on how rape survivors think about themselves, their environment, and the future. These cognitions form the cognitive triad that Beck (1972) proposed as causes of depression. One woman I treated who had been raped two years before said, "I don't know if I believe in God anymore; I don't know if I am to blame in any way for this; I don't feel like I know anything anymore! How am I supposed to get up and go to work every morning if I don't even know why I keep living?!" A number of authors have noted negative effects to victims' world of meaning (Gidycz and Koss, 1991; Janoff-Bulman, 1979; Herman, 1992; Koss and Burkhart, 1989). McCann, Sakheim, and Abrahamson (1988) proposed that symptoms will develop if the trauma disrupts prior positive schemata or seems to confirm prior negative schemata.

Longer-Term Relationship Effects

Not surprisingly, authors commonly report negative effects of rape on romantic relationships (Miller and Williams, 1984; Miller, Williams, and Bernstein, 1982; Warner, 1980). Negative effects include communication problems, mutual resentment, emotional distancing, sexual difficulties, and termination of the relationship. Some studies have also assessed the impact of rape on general social functioning and found survivors, especially if untreated, to have difficulties fulfilling their roles at work and with friends and family (Resick, Calhoun, Atkeson, and Ellis, 1981).

Longer-Term Sexual Effects

Perhaps the most pervasive longer-term effect is impaired sexual functioning or lowered sexual satisfaction. Gilbert and Cunningham (1986) reviewed the literature on postrape sexual functioning, concluding that disruption in sexual functioning is a very common sequela to rape, with the most common dysfunctions being fear of, avoidance of, or lack of desire for sex; rape victims who do not manifest actual dysfunctions tend to be less sexually satisfied following rape than other women; and some women return to their prerape levels of sexual functioning quickly but others report problems even years after the rape.

Longer-Term Spiritual Effects

Although effects on spiritual well-being following rape have not been well-studied empirically, clinical experience indicates that they can be profound. Rape survivors who previously held faith in a benevolent god or higher power sometimes lose that faith. Turning to their religious communities for support, they are sometimes further injured by people who place moral blame on victims. Herman (1992) states, "Traumatized people feel utterly abandoned, utterly alone, cast out of the human and divine systems of care and protection that sustain life" (p. 52).

Stages of Recovery

Various authors have described models of recovery from rape and other traumatic experiences (Burgess and Holmstrom, 1974; Forman, 1980; Herman, 1992; Horowitz, 1976; Koss and Harvey, 1987; Symonds, 1980). Koss and Harvey (1987) outlined a four-stage response to rape that integrates models presented by others.

The anticipatory phase is the point at which a victim begins to understand herself to be in danger, during which she may use dissociation, suppression, or other defense mechanisms or may engage in active strategizing to minimize danger. (Because this is not a stage of recovery per se, the anticipatory phase will not be discussed further.)

The impact phase includes the assault itself and the immediate aftermath. Victims generally feel intensely afraid during the assault, which often leads to deterioration and disintegration of coping responses. In the immediate aftermath, the victim may exhibit dissociative reactions, which seem to be a defense against fear and anxiety so intense as to threaten decompensation.

In the reconstitution or adjustment phase, the victim initially enters into a denial subphase. She attempts to regain a sense of control and security and to avoid reexamining her world view to accommodate the rape. A few weeks or months later, however, she is likely to develop distress symptoms again, entering a symptom formation subphase. She then might enter an anger subphase, which is the transition into the final phase. In the resolution phase, the victim seeks to discharge fully the emotional reactions to the rape and to integrate the experience.

Interventions Appropriate to Recovery Phases

Keeping in mind the contextual model of women's lives and the characteristics of each phase of recovery, we can identify a variety of interventions that might be appropriate for each of the phases.

Impact Phase Interventions. Issues regarding physical safety, emotional security and control, and relatedness are intensely salient immediately following an assault. Most models of rape treatment place safety and social support interventions as the highest priorities in this phase. Anderson and Frank (1991), reviewing recent-victim treatment studies, concluded that supportive counseling was just as effective for recent victims as cognitive behavioral interventions or systematic desensitization in terms of levels of depression, fear, anxiety, and social adjustment.

Clinical experience also suggests that interventions that assist in establishing safety and physiological and emotional equilibrium are helpful in the impact phase. Toward this end, I encourage the survivor to take actions to improve her sense of safety—seeking medical attention, staying with a friend, changing the locks on doors, reporting the assault to authorities, asking friends to accompany her when she goes out, or seeking an order of protection. The survivor may need advocacy and assistance in gathering information and taking steps to carry out these actions. It is often helpful to be directive and active with survivors in this phase, but the clinician should avoid intrusiveness that might threaten the survivor's sense of control.

At this phase, I also use containment and coping strategies to soothe and manage the stress response symptoms. I might use any of the following: relaxation training, containment imagery (the client envisions a sturdy container for the assault-related feelings and thoughts that intrude on her), soothing self-talk (that she is a strong and capable woman, that she can get through this, that she has people she can turn to for support), and making lists of healthy coping strategies (such as calling a friend, taking a walk or other exercise, doing something productive and distracting) and unhealthy strategies to avoid (such as excessive eating, casual sex, alcohol or drug use, or social withdrawal).

Adjustment Phase Interventions. During the denial subphase, the victim focuses on reclaiming her life. She attempts to return to normal, to reclaim lost activities, and to regain a sense of control in her life. Those new to working with sexual assault survivors often see this denial as unhealthy. However, it is an important part of the recovery process and should be assisted, not challenged. Specific interventions might include supporting and encouraging the survivor for being able to return to work or school, perform daily living tasks again, and tolerate situations that might remind her of the assault. Whereas in the impact phase it is appropriate to offer a lot of assistance, in the adjustment denial subphase the survivor should be encouraged to do as much on her own as possible. Deeper exploration should be avoided and is often heavily resisted by the survivor anyway.

In addition to reestablishing control, the survivor should also be encouraged to reconnect with friends and family. Communication skills training and joint sessions with supporters (if the survivor desires it) are appropriate for assisting in the reconnection process. However, the survivor is unlikely to want to talk about the rape itself at this point. Many in this adjustment phase, if they are interested in therapy at all, are concerned with how those who know about the assault think about them, how the assault is affecting their ability to relate to loved ones, or how the assault has hurt loved ones. Once they reach a tolerable equilibrium regarding security, control, and relatedness, many survivors leave treatment.

Koss and Harvey (1987) described the symptom formation subphase as commonly including "nonspecific anxiety, nightmares and fears; depression, guilt, or shame; catastrophic fantasies; feelings of vulnerability, helplessness, dirtiness, alienation, and isolation; sexual dysfunction and physical illness" (p. 36). Containment and coping strategies described for the impact phase may be useful again, with medication being appropriate when anxiety, depression, or sleep disturbances are severe. Cognitive-behavioral interventions and interpersonal therapy are effective generally with depression and are appropriate for treatment of postrape depression (Elkin and others, 1989, cited in Anderson and Frank, 1991). Regarding sexual dysfunction, Becker and Skinner (1984) outlined a ten-session sex therapy module designed for sexual assault survivors. Interventions in the adjustment subphase should be geared toward symptom management unless the survivor is ready to move into the resolution phase.

The anger subphase is the final cry of resistance to the rape, before accepting and integrating the experience. Those in this subphase want to articulate the damage that was done and hold the rapist accountable—at least in their own understanding, if not through the criminal justice system. Active listening, empty chair, art, and movement techniques are all useful at this time. The anger subphase leads into resolution and integration work as the survivor comes to full acceptance that the rape occurred and that it affected her in very profound ways.

Long-Term Resolution and Integration Therapy

Several models successful in the general treatment of trauma are applicable for work with adult survivors of rape. Models based on work with war veterans tend to focus on anxiety management during exposure to the traumatic memory (Foa, Rothbaum, Riggs, and Murdock, 1991; Horowitz, 1976), whereas psychoanalytically derived models focus on release of emotion connected with the trauma and articulation of the meaning of the trauma (Miller, 1984). Supportive treatments focus on providing a nurturing, safe relationship, which is believed to facilitate the naturally emerging processes of healing (most rape crisis centers use this model).

Herman (1992) described a model of trauma treatment that incorporates all of the above elements. She outlines three stages of recovery (or treatment): (1) reestablishing safety, (2) remembrance of the traumatic event and mourning the losses from it, and (3) reconnection with self, others, and the community. Herman's safety and reconnection components correspond with the security, control, and relatedness components of the contextual model presented earlier. The survivor's indirect style, if present, could be worked on throughout the stages as the therapist encourages the survivor to find more effective strategies to meet her needs and express her feelings. The woman-as-body concerns would probably arise in the remembrance and mourning stage as well as in the reconnection stage.

If the survivor has not yet established physical safety and sufficient psychological equilibrium by the time she seeks treatment for integration and resolution of the rape trauma, then the therapist should make those goals the first priority. The same interventions used in the impact phase and the adjustment symptom formation subphase are appropriate at this time as well. The remembrance and mourning stage of therapy requires techniques not yet discussed.

Remembrance and Mourning Stage. In this stage of therapy, the goal is to access the traumatic memories, with full attention to the factual and experiential details, including the victim's sensations, feelings, and thoughts. Psychodynamic exploration techniques and formal cognitive-behavioral exposure techniques, written or spoken, can accomplish this (Resick and Schnicke, 1992). The survivor needs to articulate her experience—at least for herself, and more ideally with the therapist or others to witness. This seems to fully ground the experience in reality, and when accomplished without the catastrophes she might have feared, provides the survivor with a sense of mastery over the experience and its aftereffects.

When the client is amnesic for some or all of the rape, other techniques might be helpful, such as bringing pictures of herself at the time of the rape to facilitate access to her awareness of herself at that age and time in her life; art, play, or movement techniques that might circumvent the usual defenses; guided imagery recall, in which the client is brought to a relaxed state and then guided to call to mind the events and asked specific details about sensory information; and hypnosis. The more intrusive techniques, especially hypnosis, should be used only after careful consideration of alternative techniques and with appropriate caution and training. Regardless of the technique used to assist remembering, it is very important to continue to use the soothing, grounding techniques of the earlier phases to help the client avoid becoming overwhelmed.

In addition to exposure to the trauma without dissociation, the client must also mourn. Mourning is the transformative process that allows the survivor to integrate the experience and move on. To facilitate mourning, the therapist should assist the client in formulating what she has lost through the experience (Herman, 1992), or precisely all that she resents about it (Miller, 1984). At this stage, denial and other defense mechanisms should be gently challenged. Psychodynamic techniques and many of the experiential techniques described earlier are useful for these goals.

Reconnection Stage. In this stage, the survivor is examining her relationship to self and others. She is developing a new lifestyle and way of thinking that incorporates all that she has learned about herself, relationships, the world, spirituality, sexuality, and other aspects of life. Herman suggests that learning to fight, reconciling with self, reconnecting to and finding a sense of commonality with others, and finding a "survivor mission" (assisting other victims or sexual assault prevention work) are all important to this stage. Assertiveness, communication, and self-defense training, as well as support or therapy groups, can facilitate these goals. Generally, once the mourning has passed, supportive, encouraging techniques are all that is required. In my experience, however, symptoms that have an addictive or self-reinforcing component do not always disappear spontaneously when the client completes the mourning. These include eating disorders, dysfunctional sexual behaviors, and alcohol and drug abuse. The therapist should target these symptoms directly throughout the treatment if possible, especially if they have not abated when the mourning stage is over.

Mediators of Recovery

There are a number of factors that can influence, if not determine, recovery from rape. These include not only the victim's preassault functioning, but also aspects of the rape itself and the victim's relationship to the perpetrator.

Prior Functioning. In addition to outlining the phases of normal recovery, authors have noted that some victims show "pathological" or compounded reactions to trauma (Gidycz and Koss, 1991). Compared to those whose recovery, though painful, is relatively uncomplicated, these victims differ primarily in terms of their preassault functioning. Because the rape (or any trauma) affects the core self, it is impossible to treat the rape effects without also treating prior traumas or maladaptive behaviors and cognition. A review of treatment techniques for all the possible preexisting psychological problems is, of course, beyond the scope of this project. Herman (1992) provides a more complete discussion of complex posttraumatic stress disorder and personality disorders associated with prolonged or repeated abuse.

Other Mediators. Gidycz and Koss found that victims who were experiencing the most postassault depression and anxiety (other than those with the poorest preassault functioning) were those who had been assaulted most forcefully and those who held sexually conservative beliefs and the belief that relationships between men and women are inherently adversarial. These beliefs may have preceded the rape or been a result of the rape. The relationship between the victim and rapist has been studied but results are inconsistent (Gidycz and Koss, 1991). However, none of this research has measured the bond felt by the victim with the rapist before the rape; I would argue that the felt bond is the relevant variable, not the outward label placed on the relationship. Level of social support following the assault has also been studied as a mediator of recovery from rape, with mixed but generally positive results— that is, the better the social support, the fewer and less severe are the symptoms (see Calhoun and Atkeson, 1991).

Support or Therapy Groups

Many of the treatment goals and techniques described above can be provided in a group format. Herman (1992) suggests psychoeducational or debriefing groups for the safety stage, a time-limited group focused on telling the story for the remembrance and mourning stage, and an interpersonal psychotherapy group for the reconnection stage. Resick and Schnicke (1992) described a group format intervention, called cognitive processing therapy, that uses both exposure and cognitive therapy components. The intervention effectively ameliorated both depressive and PTSD symptoms in women who were not incest victims and had no severe competing pathology. Cognitive processing therapy is one of very few group treatments with empirically demonstrated effectiveness in terms of postassault symptom severity (Resick and Schnicke, 1992).

Conclusion

Successful and complete treatment of adult victims of rape is a somewhat complex process, requiring knowledge of the phases of recovery from rape and techniques appropriate to each phase. However, many of the aftereffects of rape are intuitively obvious (sexual problems, fears, relationship problems, and depression) and can be further understood through consideration of the context of women's lives. Effective treatments have been developed that use an array of generally common techniques, drawn from several theoretical perspectives. Because of their eclectic nature, therapists of all backgrounds should find these treatments relatively easy to adapt and use in their own practices. Given the extremely high prevalence of childhood or adult sexual victimization among women outpatients and inpatients (see Briere, 1989), all therapists must be rape experts.

References

Anderson, B., and Frank, E. "The Efficacy of Psychological Interventions with Recent Rape Victims." In A. W. Burgess (ed.), *Rape and Sexual Assault III*. New York: Garland, 1991.

Beck, A. T. *Depression: Causes and Treatment*. Philadelphia: University of Pennsylvania Press, 1972.

Becker, J. V., and Skinner, L. J. "Behavioral Treatment of Sexual Dysfunctions in Sexual Assault Survivors." In I. R. Stuart and J. G. Greer (eds.), *Victims of Sexual Aggression: Treatment of Children, Women, and Men*. New York: Van Nostrand Reinhold, 1984.

Briere, J. *Therapy for Adults Molested as Children*. New York: Springer, 1989.

Burgess, A. W., and Holmstrom, L. L. "Rape Trauma Syndrome." *American Journal of Psychiatry*, 1974, *131*, 981–986.

Burgess, A. W., and Holmstrom, L. L. *Rape and Recovery*. Bowie, Md.: Brady, 1979.

Burgess, A. W., and Holmstrom, L. L. "Rape Trauma Syndrome and Post-Traumatic Stress Response." In A. W. Burgess (ed.), *Rape and Sexual Assault*. New York: Garland, 1985.

Burnam, M. A., and others. "Sexual Assault and Mental Disorders in a Community Population." *Journal of Consulting and Clinical Psychology*, 1988, *56*, 843–850.

Calhoun, K. S., and Atkeson, B. M. *Treatment of Rape Victims: Facilitating Psychosocial Adjustment.* Elmsford, N.Y.: Pergamon Press, 1991.

Calhoun, K. S., Atkeson, B. M., and Resick, P. A. "A Longitudinal Examination of Fear Reactions in Victims of Rape." *Journal of Counseling Psychology,* 1982, *19,* 655–661.

Ellis, E. M., Atkeson, B. M., and Calhoun, K. S. "Short Report: An Assessment of Long-Term Reaction to Rape." *Journal of Abnormal Psychology,* 1981, *90,* 263–266.

Foa, E. B., Rothbaum, B. O., Riggs, D. S., and Murdock, T. B. "Treatment of Post-Traumatic Stress Disorder in Rape Victims: A Comparison Between Cognitive-Behavioral Procedures and Counseling." *Journal of Consulting and Clinical Psychology,* 1991, *59,* 715–723.

Forman, B. "Psychotherapy with Rape Victims." *Psychotherapy: Theory, Research, and Practice,* 1980, *17,* 304–311.

Gidycz, C. A., and Koss, M. P. "Predictors of Long-Term Sexual Assault Trauma Among a National Sample of Victimized College Women." *Violence and Victims,* 1991, 175–190.

Gilbert, B. J. "Violence and the Context of Women's Lives." Unpublished manuscript, 1994.

Gilbert, B., and Cunningham, J. "Women's Post-Rape Sexual Functioning: Review and Implications for Counseling." *Journal of Counseling and Development,* 1986, *65,* 71–73.

Gilligan, C. *In a Different Voice.* Cambridge, Mass.: Harvard University Press, 1982.

Greenspan, M. *A New Approach to Women and Therapy.* New York: McGraw-Hill, 1983.

Herman, J. L. *Trauma and Recovery.* New York: Basic Books, 1992.

Horowitz, M. *Stress Response Syndromes.* New York: Jason Aronson, 1976.

Janoff-Bulman, R. "Characterological Versus Behavioral Self-Blame: Inquiries into Depression and Rape." *Journal of Personality and Social Psychology,* 1979, *37,* 1798–1809.

Kilpatrick, D. G., Resick, P. A., and Veronen, L. "Effects of a Rape Experience: A Longitudinal Study." *Journal of Social Issues,* 1981, *37,* 105–120.

Kilpatrick, D. G., Veronen, L., and Resick, P. A. "The Aftermath of Rape: Recent Empirical Findings." *American Journal of Orthopsychiatry,* 1979, *49,* 658–669.

Koss, M. P., and Burkhart, B. R. "A Conceptual Analysis of Rape Victimization: Long-Term Effects and Implications for Treatment." *Psychology of Women Quarterly,* 1989, *13,* 27–40.

Koss, M. P., and Harvey, M. R. *The Rape Victim: Clinical and Community Approaches to Treatment.* Lexington, Mass.: Stephen Greene Press, 1987.

McCann, I. L., Sakheim, D. K., and Abrahamson, D. J. "Trauma and Victimization: A Model of Psychological Adaptation." *Counseling Psychologist,* 1988, *16,* 531–594.

Miller, A. *Thou Shalt Not Be Aware: Society's Betrayal of the Child.* New York: New American Library, 1984.

Miller, W. R., and Williams, A. M. "Marital and Sexual Dysfunction Following Rape: Identification and Treatment." In I. R. Stuart and J. G. Greer (eds.), *Victims of Sexual Aggression: Treatment of Children, Women, and Men.* New York: Van Nostrand Reinhold, 1984.

Miller, W. R., Williams, A. M., and Bernstein, M. H. "The Effects of Rape on Marital and Sexual Adjustment." *American Journal of Family Therapy,* 1982, *10,* 51–58.

Notman, M. T., and Nadelson, C. C. "The Rape Victim: Psychodynamic Considerations." *American Journal of Psychiatry,* 1976, *133,* 408–412.

Resick, P. A., Calhoun, K. S., Atkeson, B. M., and Ellis, E. M. "Social Adjustment in Victims of Sexual Assault." *Journal of Consulting and Clinical Psychology,* 1981, *49* (5), 705–712.

Resick, P. A., and Schnicke, M. K. "Cognitive Processing Therapy for Sexual Assault Victims." *Journal of Consulting and Clinical Psychology,* 1992, *60,* 748–756.

Russell, D.E.H. *Sexual Exploitation: Rape, Child Sexual Abuse, and Sexual Harassment.* Newbury Park, Calif.: Sage, 1984.

Schwendinger, J. R., and Schwendinger, H. *Rape and Inequality.* Newbury Park, Calif.: Sage, 1983.

Symonds, M. "The Second Injury." In *Evaluation and Change* (Special Issue: Services to Survivors), Minnesota Medical Research Foundation, 1980.

Warner, C. G. (ed.). *Rape and Sexual Assault.* Germantown, Md.: Aspen, 1980.

BARBARA J. GILBERT, Ph.D., specializes in treatment of women who have been sexually victimized and is currently in private practice in Los Altos, California.

Effective assessment and treatment of battered women involves a
recognition of the many individual and systemic variables involved.
This chapter summarizes the major theoretical positions and research
findings and addresses their implications for treatment.

Assessing and Treating Battered Women: A Clinical Review of Issues and Approaches

Beth Houskamp

Epidemiological Findings and Definitions

Each year, domestic violence affects approximately two million marriages in the United States (Straus and Gelles, 1986). Epidemiological studies have found similar rates of violence among dating or cohabiting couples (Stets and Straus, 1989). In an analysis of National Crime Survey data, Schwartz (1987) found that in recorded cases of partner abuse involving physical injury, 95 percent of the victims who sought medical treatment were women. In their analysis of spousal homicide rates from 1976 to 1985, Mercy and Saltzman (1989) found that women were 1.3 times more at risk than their partners.

Although the vast majority of research has been conducted with primarily Caucasian samples, the problem of domestic violence is also significant in families of color. Asbury (1993) notes that the little research that exists in the area of interspousal violence among minority populations is contradictory regarding the rates of spouse abuse in different ethnic groups, particularly when socioeconomic class is controlled. However, in the few studies conducted, women of color have reported significant rates of violence by their partners, rates at least equivalent to those reported by Caucasian women (Asbury, 1993).

Abuse takes place within a context of disordered power relations, both familial and societal. The problem of violence against women is one of misuse of power, predominantly by men who believe they have the right to control women, often through the use of physical force (Walker, 1989). This misuse of power is often socially sanctioned in contemporary Western societies, with a tradition of male dominance in the family, physical strength of males, and a history of economic oppression of women (Murphy and Cascardi, 1993). Recent research has found that when men perceive themselves as having less power in the relationship, they may engage in violent behavior to compensate (Babcock, Waltz, Jacobson, and Gottman, 1993).

In a battering relationship, psychological and physical power are misused by the batterer, causing significant harm. Tolman (1992) defines psychological maltreatment as "any behavior that is harmful or intended to be harmful to the well-being of a spouse . . . [and this] negative behavior in relationships constitutes a pattern of maltreatment" (p. 292). Psychological abuse often accompanies physical abuse and usually instills fear in the victim, creates dependency on the abuser, and damages the victim's self-esteem (Murphy and Cascardi, 1993; Tolman, 1992).

There are numerous behaviors that are psychologically abusive, ranging in intensity and duration. Many women are subjected to physical threats to harm her or the children, or emotional threats to have her institutionalized or to kidnap the children. Many women also report verbal harassment and ridicule, possessive and jealous behavior, behaviors geared toward isolating her from social support, denial of access to checking accounts or finances, and rigid sex-role expectations (Follingstad and others, 1990; Tolman, 1992).

Researchers have demonstrated that exposure to domestic violence has often severe and potentially lethal physical repercussions. Physical violence has been defined as an act performed with the intention, or perceived intention, of causing physical pain or injury to another person (Hampton and Washington Coner-Edwards, 1993). Abused women often receive beatings requiring medical attention or hospitalization and many women die as a result of these assaults (Gelles and Cornell, 1985).

Before 1977, when Oregon repealed its marital exemption rule, marital rape was not a crime in the United States. Twenty years later, a number of states still have laws exempting marital rape from prosecution as sexual assault (Hampton and Washington Coner-Edwards, 1993). However, many battered women report being sexually assaulted by their partners (Finkelhor and Yllo, 1992; Shields and Hanneke, 1983). Battered women who are also raped by their partners are more likely to seek divorces and otherwise attempt to escape from the abuse (Pagelow, 1992).

Psychological Effects of Physical and Psychological Abuse

Significant psychological symptoms have been found to result from exposure to the trauma of the physical and psychological abuse of domestic violence. Many researchers have identified consistent psychological effects including symptoms of anxiety (Campbell, 1989; Walker, 1984), depression (Cascardi and O'Leary, 1992), and substance abuse (Bergman, Larsson, Brismar, and Klang, 1987).

Posttraumatic Stress Disorder. Posttraumatic stress disorder (PTSD) results from exposure to a traumatic event, such as assault, rape, or combat. Battered women have been found to fully meet diagnostic criteria for PTSD (Astin, Lawrence, and Foy, 1993; Astin, Ogland-Hand, Coleman, and Foy, in press; Houskamp and Foy, 1991; Kemp, Rawlings, and Green, 1991). The extent and severity of exposure to violence has been found to be significantly correlated with the severity of PTSD symptoms experienced (Astin, Lawrence, and Foy, 1993; Houskamp and Foy, 1991). In addition, the fact that the trauma is inflicted by a familiar person does not appear to lessen the PTSD symptoms experienced. Riggs, Kilpatrick, and Resnick (1992) found that levels of PTSD symptoms in women raped by their spouses were similar to levels of PTSD found in women who had been raped or assaulted by strangers.

Those working with battered women must also carefully attend to the battered woman's history of relationships. Studies have found that a significant percentage of battered women have a history of trauma, including childhood physical and sexual abuse (Briere and Runtz, 1987; Houskamp and Foy, 1991). Astin, Lawrence, and Foy (1993) also found that a history of childhood sexual abuse, combined with the intensity of violence in the battering relationship, significantly contributed to the degree of PTSD symptoms experienced by battered women.

Battered Woman Syndrome. Walker (1985, 1989, 1991) and others have used the term *battered woman syndrome* to describe the stress reactions experienced by many battered women. The symptoms commonly associated with battered woman syndrome include the trauma symptoms discussed above, as well as fear, depression, guilt, and low self-esteem (Douglas, 1987). Battered woman syndrome is thought to be brought on by abuse and renders the woman more able to survive the relationship but less able to leave it, due to both her belief that the relationship is inescapable and to the accompanying symptoms of trauma and stress. In addition, her coping mechanisms are impaired and the battered woman is much more likely to use self-destructive ways of coping with the abuse (Barnett and LaViolette, 1993).

Battered woman syndrome, as an expansion of the concept of legal self-defense (impaired self-defense), has been used in court to defend battered women who murder their spouses. In addition to acknowledging symptoms of trauma, the concept of battered woman syndrome hypothesizes that when someone has been repeatedly held hostage in her home, trapped, and victimized, she may respond to defend herself when there is a perceived danger, even if that danger may not appear imminent to others (O'Leary and Murphy, 1992).

Assessment and Case Management

Domestic violence against women has been a controversial area because the experience of violence over an extended period of time and within the context of a family situation is a very complex phenomenon. In order to intervene in a way that is most helpful to the battered woman, it is critical that the therapist engage in a comprehensive assessment of the battered woman's situation, beginning with an assessment of her safety and including current psychological symptoms and thorough psychological, medical, and legal histories. In addition, work with domestic violence may include case management responsibilities, many of which are often handled poorly by those without appropriate training.

As Saunders (1992) notes, domestic violence cases present many challenges to the practitioner. It can be difficult to get adequate information about the abuse. Offenders often minimize the extent of the abuse out of shame or fear of punishment. Many battered women are also reluctant to disclose the extent of the abuse. This inclination to minimize or deny symptoms fits with her perception that acknowledgment of symptoms does not carry an obvious financial, legal, or other benefit. In fact, for women still in the abusive situation, acknowledging the extent of psychological distress they are experiencing as a result of the violence may create additional unwanted internal and psychosocial conflict. In addition, there may be complex legal issues involved, such as child custody disputes, protective orders, or duty-to-warn requirements. Also, many traditional psychological assessment measures are either not useful for assessing domestic violence or are misinterpreted when used to assess battered women.

Lethality of the Relationship with the Batterer. Based on the legal decision in *Tarasoff v. Regents of the University of California* (1976), therapists have a duty to be aware of the signs of imminent danger and to warn potential victims of violent behavior threatened against them (Corey, Corey, and Callanan, 1988). However, it is difficult to accurately predict the dangerousness of the batterer. As Saunders (1992) points out, the more serious the event is (such as homicide), the more infrequently it occurs and, therefore, the more difficult it is to predict accurately. Researchers have identified several factors that appear to correlate with severe violence in male partners, including a history of severe violence in childhood, substance abuse, abuse of the children, threats to kill, and violence outside of the home (Gondolf, 1993; Saunders, 1992).

McNeill (1987) highlights critical indicators that suggest that a client with a history of abusing his partner might be currently dangerous. These factors include the extent to which the client appears to have a specific plan, whether triggering events are attached to the plan that will cause the batterer to activate it on the occurrence of some conditions, whether there has been a sudden change in the batterer's circumstances (such as job loss, divorce, infidelity of a spouse), and whether the batterer has taken any steps to activate the plan, such as purchasing a weapon or buying a plane ticket to visit the intended victim.

Protective Orders. If her physical safety is threatened and the abusive partner is threatening or otherwise harassing the battered woman, she may seek a temporary restraining order. Although protective orders do provide some measure of protection (law enforcement officers will make an arrest when called to the scene), it has been noted that many men ignore restraining orders. Many battered women are afraid to take out a protective order because they are concerned that the act of being served a restraining order will so infuriate their partner that he will hurt or kill them before the police can be called. Protective shelters may be appropriate for these women.

Child Custody. One of the great concerns for many battered women who are considering divorce is fear of losing custody of their children. Due to their exposure to trauma, during court evaluations battered women may appear more psychologically dysfunctional than their abusers. The growing movement in the courts toward joint custody, even when one spouse has strong objections because of abuse, terrifies many battered women (Pagelow, 1992). Custody arrangements often become an additional means for the abuser to maintain power, domination, and control over the battered woman. Children of men who batter their spouses are also at risk of being abused, and battered women often fear leaving their children with the abuser (Pagelow, 1992; Walker, 1984).

Assessment of Psychological Functioning

Assessment measures can provide useful information regarding the nature of the abuse, the possible dangerousness of the situation, and the effects of the trauma on the battered woman. The Conflict Tactics Scale-Revised (CTS-R) (Hornung, McCullough, and Sugimoto, 1981) has been found to provide a reliable and valid measure of exposure to violence (Barling and others, 1987). Several items are often added when the CTS-R is used clinically or in research; these added items usually assess physically and psychologically abusive incidents such as forced sexual contact, use of a knife or gun, or threats to harm or take away the children (Houskamp and Foy, 1991; Saunders, 1992).

Assessment of the battered woman's psychological functioning is a controversial area. Common psychological measures used by court examiners, such as the Minnesota Multiphasic Personality Inventory (MMPI), can be easily misused to present battered women as pathological (for example, in court evaluations for custody). Recent studies are demonstrating more accurate interpretations of results of personality measures such as the MMPI (Rosewater, 1988; Rhodes, 1992). However, the MMPI and other standardized personality measures are not the most useful and accurate in assessing battered women's psychological functioning; if they are used, the interpretation must be based on a comprehensive knowledge of the interactive effect of exposure to trauma and scores on these standardized measures.

A more precise approach to assessing psychological symptoms in battered women is to use measures specifically designed to assess trauma symptoms. The Impact of Event Scale (Horowitz, Wilner, and Alvarez, 1979) assesses avoidant and intrusive symptomatology and has been helpful in assessing symptoms of posttraumatic stress. More recently, Briere (in press) has developed the Trauma Symptom Inventory, a measure used to assess symptoms such as posttraumatic stress, anger, dissociation, anxiety, depression, and disrupted self-capacities. Although this measure has not yet been used in research specifically with battered women, it provides a comprehensive assessment of critical sequelae not covered by other measures and should prove to be very useful in assessing trauma symptoms in battered women.

Finally, a good clinical interview is essential to accurately assess the psychological functioning of battered women. A clinical interview should include a thorough psychological history, medical history, and abuse history, including a history of any physical or sexual abuse in childhood or adulthood and an assessment of the number, severity, and any precipitating factors of abusive incidents. Throughout the interview, questions must be as specific as possible in order to assist the battered woman in giving an accurate picture of both the incidents that have occurred and her psychological response. Many women might not consider psychological abuse or marital rape to be abusive compared to the severe physical beatings they might also have experienced.

Treatment Approaches and Modalities

In light of the complexities of domestic violence against women, effective treatment of battered women must be based on a comprehensive assessment of the situation and demands a thorough knowledge of alternative treatment modalities. Treatment planning must include a means of addressing the dynamics of the violent relationship as well as helping the battered woman work through the sequelae of trauma she may be experiencing. Often several different treatment modalities may be necessary in order to best assist the battered woman.

Family or Couple Therapy. One of the most controversial treatment debates has been over the appropriateness of marital or family therapy for treatment of domestic violence. Although court-ordered therapy for spouse battering has become more widespread, if the modality is not specified in the court order, the couple will often present together asking for assistance with "their" problems. However, family systems approaches to working with domestic violence have been the object of significant criticism and concern (Bograd, 1984; Gondolf, 1993).

A primary concern is the issue of safety. Many battered women fear reprisals from the batterer and are therefore hesitant to confront him or attend marital sessions with him (Gondolf, 1993). Because of her fear and accompanying dissociation, the battered woman may have difficulty attending to the session with her abuser in the room (Bograd, 1984; Walker, 1989). If the woman does feel safe enough in the session to describe his violence and her emotional experience of it, she is often punished for it later (Barnett and LaViolette, 1993).

In addition, it is often difficult to establish a working therapeutic alliance with the abusive spouse; batterers often resist taking responsibility, deny they have a problem, seek control of the sessions, and project blame onto their partner (Bograd, 1984). His violence must be the focus of treatment, a treatment goal that usually meets with considerable resistance. However, family systems approaches tend to overlook power issues and to focus on the underlying systemic dysfunction, and clinicians may minimize the violence as they address concerns over parenting, communication, or other marital issues (Bograd, 1984).

Experts working with battered women and with abusive men generally recommend structuring therapeutic modalities with individual or group therapy as the primary mode of treatment. Court-ordered programs are increasingly moving toward group therapy as the modality of choice for working with batterers (Gondolf, 1993). After the abusive partner has adequately acknowledged responsibility for his abusive behavior and safety in the relationship has been firmly established, if both partners are amenable, a modification of marital therapy, with multiple therapists involved, may be appropriate (Gondolf, 1993; Walker, 1989).

Therapy for the Battered Woman. Effective therapy for battered women offers a supportive relationship that validates the woman's perceptions, encourages self-determination, and provides a safe setting to work through the residue of years of trauma. Therapy may include supporting the battered woman as she addresses decisions such as whether to permanently or temporarily leave the relationship, to file for divorce, to obtain a restraining order, or to locate employment or child care (Dutton-Douglas, 1992). Although both individual and group therapy have been found to be effective, group therapy and self-help groups provide an additional avenue of social support and healing that can be critical to the often isolated battered woman. Many therapists recognize that a support group may be the only means of healing some battered women, and recommend that if a battered woman is in individual therapy, she also join a local support group (Dutton-Douglas, 1992; Walker, 1989).

Abuse-Focused Therapy. In order to fully recover from the experience of being battered, many battered women need to address the traumatic effects of victimization. Dutton-Douglas (1992) notes that this work can occur only after the threat of continued abuse has ceased, and highlights four components of recovering from the trauma of battery. These phases are similar to those addressed in abuse-focused therapy with adult survivors of child abuse and other trauma groups, and much of what is introduced here can be further explored through a study of the general literature on adult survivors of trauma.

First, Dutton-Douglas (1992) stresses the importance of working through the trauma. Included in this phase is the lessening of emotional numbing and avoidance by naming the traumatic event and incorporating journaling, imagery, or body work into the therapy in order to work through the traumatic experiences. In addition, Dutton-Douglas (1992) emphasizes the importance of developing strategies to cope with intrusive symptoms such as nightmares and flashbacks. Relaxation techniques, stress management strategies, and emphasizing self-care and nurturing of the self can assist the battered woman in coping. Ultimately, the goal of the working-through phase of treatment is to integrate the trauma into the former battered woman's everyday life, thereby empowering her to move forward with her life (Barnett and LaViolette, 1993; Dutton-Douglas, 1992).

The second phase of abuse-focused treatment involves addressing symptom patterns associated with victimization, such as eating and sleep problems, dissociation, memory impairment, paranoid thinking, anxiety, substance abuse, and low self-esteem. It is useful to point out to the battered woman that these problems are normal reactions to trauma (Dutton-Douglas, 1992). A critical aspect of this phase of the treatment process is intervening in the battered woman's impaired identity and self-reference. Many battered women, particularly those with a history of abuse in childhood as well as adulthood, struggle with an impaired sense of self. Extended, intensive therapy appears to have a significant and enduring impact on abuse survivors' sense of selfhood (Briere, 1992; McCann and Pearlman, 1990).

The third phase of treatment concerns changing dysfunctional cognitions. This phase includes focusing on the basic human right not to be abused, the right to experience one's feelings, and the right to control one's body (Dutton-Douglas, 1992; Walker, 1991). A critical aspect of this phase of therapy is to increase the battered woman's ability to distinguish what she can control (her own behavior) from what she cannot (her partner's violence).

Finally, the battered woman needs to move on with her life, including developing strategies for maintaining good boundaries and identifying areas where she may be at risk for future victimization. If couple therapy is an option for the battered woman and her partner has successfully completed his individual treatment, conjoint work might be a useful adjunct for the couple at this time (Dutton-Douglas, 1992).

Community Prevention Programs. Ultimately, intervention in spouse abuse must include work on a societal level to change the social forces that contribute to violence against women (Murphy and Meyer, 1991; Walker, 1989). Education through public service announcements and documentaries appears to have raised consciousness regarding domestic violence (Barnett and LaViolette, 1993). School programs have been found to be effective in changing attitudes toward women and domestic violence (Jaffe, Suderman, Reitzel, and Killip, 1992). Churches have also been identified as a key initial resource for many battered women in crisis. Fortune (1991) has published an extensive workshop curriculum designed for training clergy and others working in a religious context to better respond to issues of domestic violence.

Conclusion

The current literature provides direction in the documentation of the problem of domestic violence and the assessment of trauma sequelae in battered women. In the past twenty years, the importance of a systemic response that includes the judicial system and community support groups has been recognized. However, there is much unexplored territory. In particular, there is a great need for development of abuse-focused treatment approaches specifically designed to address the complexities of working with the ongoing trauma of abusive relationships in adulthood. In addition, a paucity of research exists in the area of domestic violence against women of color and the impact cultural issues may have on the therapy process for these women. Finally, there is continued need for those working with domestic violence to work on a societal level to better prevent and ultimately eliminate the societal attitudes and behavior that contribute to violence against women.

References

Asbury, J. "Violence in Families of Color in the United States." In R. Hampton and others (eds.), *Family Violence: Prevention and Treatment.* Newbury Park, Calif.: Sage, 1993.

Astin, M. C., Lawrence, K. J., and Foy, D. W. "Posttraumatic Stress Disorder Among Battered Women: Risk and Resiliency Factors." *Violence and Victims,* 1993, *8* (1), 17–28.

Astin, M. C., Ogland-Hand, S. M., Coleman, E. M., and Foy, D. W. "Posttraumatic Stress Disorder in Battered Women: Comparisons with Maritally Distressed Women." *Journal of Consulting and Clinical Psychology,* in press.

Babcock, J. C., Waltz, J., Jacobson, N. S., and Gottman, J. M. "Power and Violence: The Relation Between Communication Patterns, Power Discrepancies, and Domestic Violence." *Journal of Consulting and Clinical Psychology,* 1993, *61* (1), 40–50.

Barling, J., O'Leary, K. D., Jouriles, E. N., Vivian, D., and MacEwen, K. E. "Factor Similarity of the Conflict Tactics Scale Across Samples, Spouses, and Sites: Issues and Implications." *Journal of Family Violence,* 1987, *2* (1), 37–54.

Barnett, O. W., and LaViolette, A. D. *It Could Happen to Anyone: Why Battered Women Stay.* Newbury Park, Calif.: Sage, 1993.

Bergman, B., Larsson, G., Brismar, B., and Klang, M. "Psychiatric Morbidity and Personality Characteristics of Battered Women." *Acta Psychiatric Scandinavica,* 1987, *76,* 678–683.

Bograd, M. "Family Systems Approaches to Wife Beating: A Feminist Critique." *American Journal of Orthopsychiatry,* 1984, *54* (4), 558–568.

Briere, J. *Child Abuse Trauma: Theory and Treatment of the Lasting Effects.* Newbury Park, Calif.: Sage, 1992.

Briere, J. *Professional Manual for the Trauma Symptom Inventory.* Odessa, Fla.: Psychological Assessment Resources, in press.

Briere, J., and Runtz, M. "Post-Sexual-Abuse Trauma: Data and Implications for Clinical Practice." *Journal of Interpersonal Violence,* 1987, *2,* 367–379.

Campbell, J. C. "Women's Responses to Sexual Abuse in Intimate Relationships." *Health Care for Women International,* 1989, *8,* 335–347.

Cascardi, M., and O'Leary, K. D. "Depressive Symptomatology, Self-Esteem, and Self Blame in Battered Women." *Journal of Family Violence,* 1992, *7,* 249–259.

Corey, G., Corey, M. S., and Callanan, P. *Issues and Ethics in the Helping Professions.* (3rd ed.) Pacific Grove, Calif.: Brooks/Cole, 1988.

Douglas, M. A. "Battered Woman Syndrome." In D. J. Sonkin (ed.), *Domestic Violence on Trial: Psychological and Legal Dimensions of Family Violence.* New York: Springer, 1987.

Dutton-Douglas, M. A. "Treating Battered Women in the Aftermath Stage." *Psychotherapy in Independent Practice,* 1992, *10* (1–2), 91–98.

Finkelhor, D., and Yllo, K. "Forced Sex in Marriage: A Preliminary Research Report." *Crime and Delinquency,* 1992, *82,* 459–478.

Follingstad, D. R., Rutledge, L. L., Berg, B. J., Hause, E. S., and Polek, D. S. "The Role of Emotional Abuse in Physically Abusive Relationships." *Journal of Family Violence*, 1990, 5, 107–120.

Fortune, M. M. *Violence in the Family: A Workshop Curriculum for Clergy and Other Helpers.* Cleveland: Pilgrim Press, 1991.

Gelles, R. J., and Cornell, C. P. *Intimate Violence in Families.* Newbury Park, Calif.: Sage, 1985.

Gondolf, E. W. "Male Batterers." In R. Hampton, T. Gullotta, G. Adams, E. Potter, and R. Weissberg (eds.), *Family Violence: Prevention and Treatment.* Newbury Park, Calif.: Sage, 1993.

Hampton, R. L., and Washington Coner-Edwards, A. F. "Physical and Sexual Violence in Marriage." In R. Hampton, T. Gullotta, G. Adams, E. Potter, and R. Weissberg (eds.), *Family Violence: Prevention and Treatment.* Newbury Park, Calif.: Sage, 1993.

Hornung, C. A., McCullough, B. C., and Sugimoto, T. "Status Relationships in Marriage: Risk Factors in Spouse Abuse." *Journal of Marriage and the Family*, 1981, 43, 675–692.

Horowitz, M. J., Wilner, N., and Alvarez, W. "Impact of Event Scale: A Measure of Subject Stress." *Psychosomatic Medicine*, 1979, 41, 209–218.

Houskamp, B. M., and Foy, D. W. "The Assessment of Posttraumatic Stress Disorder in Battered Women." *Journal of Interpersonal Violence*, 1991, 6, 367–375.

Jaffe, P. G., Suderman, M., Reitzel, D., and Killip, S. M. "An Evaluation of a Secondary School Primary Prevention Program on Violence in Intimate Relationships." *Violence and Victims*, 1992, 7, 129–146.

Kemp, A., Rawlings, E. I., and Green, B. L. "Post-Traumatic Stress Disorder (PTSD) in Battered Women: A Shelter Sample." *Journal of Traumatic Stress*, 1991, 4, 137–148.

McCann, I. L., and Pearlman, L. A. *Psychological Trauma and the Adult Survivor: Theory, Therapy, and Transformation.* New York: Brunner/Mazel, 1990.

McNeill, M. "Domestic Violence: The Skeleton in Tarasoff's Closet." In D. J. Sonkin (ed.), *Domestic Violence on Trial: Psychological and Legal Dimensions of Family Violence.* New York: Springer, 1987.

Mercy, J. A., and Saltzman, L. E. "Fatal Violence Among Spouses in the United States, 1976–1985." *American Journal of Public Health*, 1989, 79, 595–599.

Murphy, C. M., and Cascardi, M. "Psychological Aggression and Abuse in Marriage." In R. Hampton, T. Gullotta, G. Adams, E. Potter, and R. Weissberg (eds.), *Family Violence: Prevention and Treatment.* Newbury Park, Calif.: Sage, 1993.

Murphy, C. M., and Meyer, S. "Gender, Power, and Violence in Marriage." *Behavior Therapist*, 1991, 14, 95–100.

O'Leary, K. D., and Murphy, C. M. "Clinical Issues in the Assessment of Spouse Abuse." In R. T. Ammerman and M. Herson (eds.), *Assessment of Family Violence.* New York: Wiley, 1992.

Pagelow, M. D. "Adult Victims of Domestic Violence." *Journal of Interpersonal Violence*, 1992, 7, 87–120.

Rhodes, N. R. "Comparison of MMPI Psychopathic Deviate Scores of Battered and Nonbattered Women." *Journal of Family Violence*, 1992, 7 (4), 297–307.

Riggs, D. S., Kilpatrick, D. G., and Resnick, H. S. "Long-Term Psychological Distress Associated with Marital Rape and Aggravated Assault: A Comparison to Other Crime Victims." *Journal of Family Violence*, 1992, 7, 283–296.

Rosewater, L. B. "Battered or Schizophrenic? Psychological Tests Can't Tell." In K. Yllo and M. Bograd (eds.), *Feminist Perspectives on Wife Abuse.* Newbury Park, Calif.: Sage, 1988.

Saunders, D. G. "Woman Battering." In R. T. Ammerman and M. Herson (eds.), *Assessment of Family Violence.* New York: Wiley, 1992.

Schwartz, M. D. "Gender and Injury in Spousal Assault." *Sociological Focus*, 1987, 20, 61–74.

Shields, N. M., and Hanneke, C. R. "Battered Wives' Reactions to Marital Rape." In D. Finkelhor, R. J. Gelles, and G. T. Hotaling (eds.), *The Dark Side of Families: Current Family Violence Research.* Newbury Park, Calif.: Sage, 1983.

Stets, J. A., and Straus, M. A. "The Marriage License as a Hitting License: A Comparison of Assaults in Dating, Cohabitating, and Married Couples." *Journal of Family Violence*, 1989, *4*, 161–180.

Straus, M., and Gelles, R. "Social Change and Change in Family Violence from 1971 to 1985 as Revealed by Two National Surveys." *Journal of Marriage and the Family*, 1986, *48*, 465–479.

Tolman, R. M. "Psychological Abuse of Women." In R. T. Ammerman and M. Herson (eds.), *Assessment of Family Violence: A Clinical and Legal Sourcebook*. New York: Wiley, 1992.

Walker, L. E. *The Battered Woman Syndrome*. New York: Springer, 1984.

Walker, L. E. "Psychological Impact of the Criminalization of Domestic Violence on Victims." *Victimology: An International Journal*, 1985, *10* (1–4), 281–300.

Walker, L. E. "Psychology and Violence Against Women." *American Psychologist*, 1989, *44* (4), 695–702.

Walker, L. E. "Post-Traumatic Stress Disorder in Women: Diagnosis and Treatment of Battered Woman Syndrome." *Psychotherapy*, 1991, *28*, 21–29.

BETH HOUSKAMP, Ph.D., is associate professor of marital and family therapy at Azusa Pacific University.

Sexual abuse survivors often present with a complex and changing symptom picture in which posttraumatic reactions are superimposed on an underlying personality disorder, a combination that makes the establishment of a secure therapeutic relationship difficult. An eclectic blend of principles and techniques is recommended in order to address both aspects of the survivor's disturbance.

Treating Survivors of Child Sexual Abuse: A Strategy for Reintegration

Karin C. Meiselman

Child sexual abuse has been recognized as a major etiological factor in the development of adult psychopathology only within the past fifteen years. Therefore, it is not surprising that the formulation of treatment principles for survivors began only about ten years ago. Noteworthy contributors in this regard include Herman (1981), Gelinas (1983), Courtois (1988), Gil (1988), Briere (1989, 1992), and Meiselman (1990). Although the treatment field is still young, there is a comfortable sense of convergence in regard to the basic guidelines of therapy, with some inevitable disagreement about specific methods of treatment. This chapter summarizes what I believe to be the consensus of experts in the field.

Diagnostic Conceptualization: Reintegration Therapy

Psychotherapy for adults molested as children is often an unusually complex and challenging enterprise. Not only are there likely to be a number of the problems described by Neumann (Chapter Three, this volume) and Elliott (Chapter One, this volume), but the symptom picture may change abruptly as intrusion of trauma-related material alternates with periods of avoidance. Episodes of self-destructive behavior may augment the perceived difficulty of such cases to the point where psychotherapist burnout becomes a serious concern. Addressing the symptoms manifested by an individual survivor is not enough. Central to conducting psychotherapy is an understanding of how sexually abused clients have been damaged before, during, and after the sexual abuse itself, such that they are generally not a case of "simple PTSD."

Children who are inadequately nurtured and protected by their families are thought to be more vulnerable to both incest and extrafamilial sexual abuse

(Finkelhor, 1984). Especially in father-daughter incest, the absence of a nurturing bond between mother and daughter in the presence of an abusive father may put the child at serious risk. A child's early experience in such families may often be sufficient to produce a personality disorder whether or not sexual abuse actually occurs (Briere, 1992), and a dysfunctional family may compound the trauma when the child victim discloses by reacting with denial or punishment (Courtois, 1988).

Unresolved traumatic experiences can result in chronic or delayed post-traumatic stress disorder. Sometimes knowledge about the traumatic event has been repressed and the PTSD symptoms appear meaningless, even psychotic; perhaps more commonly, memory for the affect generated by abuse may be unavailable, and the survivor has minimal understanding of the relationship between abuse experiences and symptom formation. Especially in cases of repetitive abuse, habitual dissociative defenses may be established, and these defenses become maladaptive outside of the abuse situation (Gelinas, 1983).

A third type of damage that may further complicate the symptom picture is revictimization, both physical and sexual, by other perpetrators. There is a strong association between child sexual abuse and other types of trauma occurring in adolescence and adulthood (Russell, 1986), possibly due to the child's accommodation to the first victimization. This means that for many survivors the original trauma is compounded with possible augmentation of PTSD symptoms and negative self-concept.

Effective psychotherapy must address not only the sexual abuse and any subsequent trauma from revictimization, but in many cases must also create a stable therapeutic alliance with a client who lacks the early attachment experiences that allow for trust and intimacy in adulthood. Traditional schools of therapy offer ideas about how to confront some aspects of this complex treatment challenge, but none seems adequate by itself. What is needed is an eclectic blend that draws heavily on trauma theory but also uses some of the more traditional techniques associated with gradual personality change during longer-term therapy. I have recently suggested (Meiselman, 1990) that this treatment approach be called reintegration therapy.

The goal of reintegration therapy is to reconnect remembered traumatic events with their associated affects and to allow any unremembered traumatic events to surface and be placed into the context of the survivor's emotional reactions. The negative effects of the trauma can then be traced to their original source so that the survivor can now understand emotional reactions previously attributed to "badness" or "craziness." As a result of this reintegration process, the survivor can realign existing relationships by assuming a more adult, present-oriented role with significant others. Reintegration therapy can be seen as having three major tasks that tend to occur in chronological order: establishment of the client-therapist relationship, allowing repressed memories and affects into consciousness, and realigning current relationships.

Building the Therapeutic Relationship

Working on unresolved trauma requires that a survivor at least partially reexperience affects that were too painful and terrifying to be processed in a normal manner at the time of the abuse. To accomplish this task, the survivor must develop a secure base (Bowlby, 1988) of trust in the therapist and the consequent expectation of being helped to handle the pain of confronting the trauma. Unfortunately, establishing this secure base—or anchor, as some survivors call it—is often challenging with severely abused clients, especially those from dysfunctional families in which the child had no dependable, nurturing relationships. Though not always apparent on first contact, the distrust and guardedness of these survivors can be profound, and often require an extended period of careful therapeutic work before even a modicum of trust develops. This relationship-building phase is crucial to eventual success.

Assessment Phase: Evaluating Sexual Abuse History. Establishing rapport and a sense of personal security is first priority during the initial session, as is addressing any immediate crisis that may have precipitated therapeutic contact. When taking a personal history, it is important to assess the major background factors known to be associated with psychological disturbance in adults. Given the accumulating evidence that child sexual abuse is one of these factors, omitting it from an evaluation is not good practice. However, given the recent criticism (Loftus, 1993) of therapists specializing in adult survivors as being overly intent on finding sexual abuse, it behooves us to think carefully about the manner and timing of our inquiry.

During initial history taking, questions about sexual abuse should be embedded in the larger context of questions about the client's family of origin, relationship with parents and siblings, health, and educational history. In this manner, the question is a natural part of the personal history assessment and does not suggest to the client that the therapist weighs this factor much more heavily than others. It is also advisable to avoid words such as *abuse, incest, rape,* and even *molest* while inquiring about child sexual abuse history because the survivor may never have connected these concepts with his or her personal experience. Instead, one can pose questions such as, "When you were a child, were you ever approached in a sexual manner?" or "Have you ever had sexual contact with someone more than five years older than yourself?"

When a client gives a history of child sexual abuse, one can then inquire about aspects of the abuse that may be associated with the seriousness of the trauma, such as the nature of the sexual acts, the frequency and duration of abuse, the use of threats and violence, and the response of significant others to disclosure of the abuse. Although it is desirable to assess these factors as early as possible in therapy, basic clinical judgment must be used in deciding whether the survivor is ready to talk about details of sexual abuse and the emotions experienced at the time, especially because many survivors report that they have *never* told anyone and that breaking the silence is very frightening. Some survivors, in fact, will deny abuse experiences when initially asked and disclose them only after testing the therapist's trustworthiness over a period of time.

Whenever a survivor discloses sexual abuse, the therapist's ability to simply listen in a calm, empathic manner is paramount, especially because many survivors have experienced withdrawal, denial, or even punishment from significant others. After disclosure, some reassurance on the order of "I'm very sorry that that happened to you!" and "Thank you for sharing that with me!" may be advisable, and in some instances therapists may want to express the idea that perpetrators are always responsible for engaging a younger, less powerful partner in sexual activity, whether or not force or deadly threats were used. However, a very immediate, emphatic insistence that the survivor was not to blame may be contraindicated because some survivors interpret this stance as forbidding exploration of their feelings of guilt and shame. Also, it is a therapeutic error to express extreme anger at the perpetrator because many survivors have also perpetrated against others, especially in childhood and adolescence. Also, many harbor unexpressed feelings of affection and loyalty toward their own perpetrator, especially when he or she was a source of nurturance.

Working on the Client's Immediate Agenda. It is rare for the adult survivor to enter therapy with the specific goal of working through unresolved child sexual abuse. Usually, the survivor's equilibrium has been recently disrupted by problems with current relationships. This is his or her immediate agenda, and a therapist-directed focus on the sexual abuse history would jeopardize rapport. Although assessment of the client's sexual abuse history may have raised suspicions about the possible role of sexual abuse trauma in his or her current difficulties, it is usually advisable to initiate therapy by accepting any realistic goals that the client suggests.

There is no one therapeutic technique that must be used with survivors. Cognitive-behavioral, psychodynamic, rational-emotive, feminist, Gestalt, and many other therapeutic approaches can be employed productively, provided that the therapist maintains the flexibility to work on the "here and now" and to move whenever indicated to the "there and then" of sexual abuse and other significant formative events. For instance, the immediate problem of a marital crisis could be addressed with many different therapeutic techniques, depending on the training and personal style of the therapist. If the crisis resolves as a result of the initial intervention, there may not be any need to explore the possible connections with sexual abuse trauma. The repeated failure of brief interventions points to the importance of exploring the client's early emotional conditioning. The client may also become aware of emotional reactions to current problems that are markedly out of proportion. Discovery of such under- or overreactions often leads to deeper therapeutic work that, almost of necessity, involves an exploration of the survivor's emotional history.

Caring for the Client. Clients with traumatic histories are unlikely to develop a strong therapeutic bond with a therapist who appears remote and uninvolved. Effective therapy requires that the client be soothed and actively helped to weather the feelings of terror and rage that threaten to break through when the trauma is approached. Without such support, the client may leave therapy abruptly or remain at an impasse. Cultivating a sense of empathic caring for the client and being "real" with the client, engaging in carefully limited types of self-disclosure, are therefore recommended.

While caring for the client, the therapist must gently but firmly maintain the professional boundaries of the client-therapist relationship. The therapist should see caring as an attitude of positive support within the necessary confines of a professional relationship, not as a willingness to "go all out" for the survivor by bending the rules a bit further with each crisis until the therapist has been drawn into an untenable position. It is not unusual, for instance, to hear of situations in which a therapist has gradually extended session time such that an office visit can become an open-ended marathon. No matter how "manipulative" a client may be, it is the therapist who bears the ultimate responsibility for maintaining therapeutic boundaries. Especially in the case of incest survivors, who have been traumatized in the context of warped familial roles, stepping outside appropriate boundaries to become the client's friend or lover will result in a miscarriage of therapy.

Within the therapeutic hour, caring for the client can occur in a manner that does not create an undue expectation of a personal relationship. Mirroring, to a limited extent, the client's affective state, demonstrating accurate empathy through reflections, and engaging in selective self-disclosures are all techniques that enhance a client's sense of being understood. Reassurance that is honest, rather global, and given *after* the client has been given an opportunity to express his or her feelings, can contribute to a sense of being cared for and protected. For some clients, relaxation and guided imagery of a positive nature enhances the sense of nurturance in therapy.

Given that the sexually abused client receives caring, consistent therapy, the stage has been set for working on any unresolved trauma issues. However, many survivors repeatedly test the client-therapist bond by missing appointments, acting out, and making conscious or unconscious attempts to distort the therapeutic relationship. When the course of therapy becomes a test of the therapist's maturity, it is well to remember that the survivor oscillates between attachment and distrust for very understandable reasons. Therapeutic attention to trauma can result in periods of depression or anxiety—affects that the survivor defends against with denial or reinstitution of primitive avoidance strategies such as self-mutilation, drug or alcohol abuse, or compulsive sexuality. In addition, many survivors have never experienced consistent nurturance, and their profound distrust is periodically aroused as the therapeutic relationship develops, resulting in abrupt withdrawal from therapy or sudden hostility that serves to distance the therapist.

Avoiding Coercive Measures. Sexually abused persons have experienced some form of coercion, whether violence, threats, or misuse of authority, and they are therefore sensitized to any aspect of therapy that might recapitulate the abuse situation. Many times it is impossible to avoid wounding the client because the ordinary limits and boundaries that must be maintained in therapy are interpreted as coercion. However, one should strive to eliminate coercive measures that are, in reality, punishment of the client for not carrying out the therapist's wishes, such as threatening to terminate therapy if the client does not go through with a divorce.

Because sexual abuse survivors are often suicidal, the question of hospitalization can easily arise; much less frequently, abuse-related rage can emerge, accompanied by threats to harm others. In some jurisdictions, the therapist may be required to make a child abuse report, even in cases where the abuse described by the client occurred many years ago. In all of these situations, the likelihood that coercive measures must be taken can be minimized by notifying the client of the circumstances that would require them. For instance, when the client is expressing suicidal ideation, the therapist can clarify the criteria for seeking an involuntary psychiatric admission, thus giving the client the choice of whether to divulge information that might precipitate coercive action. A secondary benefit of providing such information is to create a more secure atmosphere for the client to work on suicidal feelings and ideation that fall below the threshold for authoritarian measures.

Return of Repressed Memories and Affects

Derepression can be spontaneous and is sometimes precipitated before therapy in response to life events, especially those that share key elements with the original trauma. A new trauma, such as rape or spousal abuse, may lower the survivor's defenses while simultaneously stimulating the memory of earlier episodes of abuse. It is not unusual for victims of crimes to report that they suddenly recall childhood events that they had not remembered for many years. These events typically resemble the crime and its aftermath in some manner, in either emotional or factual content. In addition, milestone events in life such as marriage, death of the perpetrator, or a child reaching the age when the survivor was abused, can sometimes create the conditions for derepression.

Derepression can also take place as a natural part of psychotherapy. As the therapeutic bond becomes firmly established, it provides the security the survivor requires in order to gradually let go of defenses that were established to handle overwhelming childhood situations, most prominently repression and dissociation. This process may be responsible for the adage that clients often get worse before they get better during longer-term therapy; periods of depression, anxiety, acting out, and renewed testing of the client-therapist bond are often reported during a derepression process.

Some psychotherapeutic techniques are thought to stimulate derepression. Perhaps the simplest of these uncovering techniques is to pose the question, "Can you think of other times in your life when you have felt this way?" after the client has described and at least partially entered into the affective state of a current life situation. This question may be most relevant when the level and type of affective response does not seem to correspond to the superficial reality of the situation. Encouraging exploration of the history and meaning of current problems—such as obesity, sexual dysfunction, or self-injurious behavior—works in a similar fashion to encourage recall of emotionally significant events, whether or not these events have been repressed.

Groups for survivors of child sexual abuse may also stimulate derepression experiences (Herman and Schatzow, 1987). Hearing other survivors tell of their abuse experiences and associated emotional states may trigger memories that have been kept out of the client's consciousness by avoidance of their associations. For instance, a survivor who has suppressed the knowledge of a rape may have established a strong avoidance of any mention of the word, newspaper reports of crime, or even consideration of self-defense strategies. However, if the survivor is able to commit to group attendance, exposure to the long-avoided stimuli is inevitable, and these stimuli may pull their associations from his or her memory.

A more concrete exploration of the survivor's childhood environment may also stimulate derepression. Visiting a childhood home, talking with people who were present during that period of life, and going through family photo albums and memorabilia are all ways of reviving memories that may be connected with currently unremembered events. When there is no actual place to revisit, forming a vivid mental image of a place well-known in the past—for example, the kitchen of the house where the survivor lived when he or she was in elementary school—may pull associated memories of childhood experience.

The use of hypnosis for exploration of childhood memories is controversial. Dolan (1991) has described numerous techniques that may be used by a therapist with specific training and supervision in hypnosis. Although recall may be stimulated by hypnotically enhancing the vividness of an already-remembered scene, survivors must be informed that hypnosis is not a magic key to discovering and validating memories. Attempting to greatly accelerate the pace of derepression through hypnosis or any other method should be discouraged.

Many other uncovering techniques may be productively used with sexual abuse survivors. Dream analysis, psychodrama, and art or movement therapy may be recommended, depending on the client's preferred style of self-expression. The most important principle is to involve the survivor in actively choosing the technique and to pay close attention to both verbal and behavioral cues from the client that suggest that he or she is not yet ready to intensify exploration. The therapist should expect to see the client oscillate between approach to the memory and protective denial. Although it can be frustrating to sense that the survivor is retreating just as he or she appears to be on the verge of a major breakthrough, the client should be allowed to go at his or her own pace throughout the process of trauma resolution. A therapist's proper role is to encourage, not to push.

There are some other cautions in doing trauma work with sexual abuse survivors. The therapist must be prepared to handle strong abreactions yet avoid predicting that they will occur or continue. Although some survivors will recall a traumatic event and its associated affect suddenly, this is not the goal of therapy. It is best to communicate to the client that derepression is a gradual process in which bits and pieces of memory and affect are mastered as the strength of his or her adult personality grows. Much too often, sexual abuse survivors have acquired the unrealistic expectation that one key memory will emerge in a very dramatic, abreactive manner and that their problems will then resolve easily.

Similarly, it is important to give survivors the message that they need not remember every last detail of their trauma in order to begin their healing process in the present. Sometimes the visual image of a jigsaw puzzle with regard to the emotional landscape of childhood trauma is helpful. Looking at the individual pieces of a puzzle yields little information, but as more pieces are found and fitted together, the overall pattern of the puzzle emerges, and if some individual pieces are still missing, they make little difference in understanding the overall picture. In this manner, the survivor is given permission not to engage in an obsessive search to know everything.

Perhaps the most important caution in guiding a client through the derepression process is to resist the client's attempts to get the therapist to validate any memories that have emerged. Traumatic memories are commonly accompanied by conflicts about the reality of what has been remembered, and the client may demand that the therapist resolve these conflicts by telling him or her "what is real." Even in instances where the memory fits in well with other established facts about the survivor's background and helps to make sense of unusual emotional responses, the fact remains that only the survivor can make the decision to believe or disbelieve the new memory.

Realignment of Significant Relationships

When the sexual abuse survivor has established a client-therapist bond that has allowed him or her to gradually address unresolved trauma, progress on improving current relationships often becomes evident. The client who dropped out of an assertiveness training group or reached an impasse in sex therapy, for instance, may now work productively with these therapeutic modalities; the sexually harassed employee may stand up for his or her rights; the ineffective parent may become open to learning new methods of discipline; and the survivor may finally reach a level of inner security that allows him or her to confront the perpetrator or significant others who failed to protect.

Confrontation of others, especially a known perpetrator, should not be held out to the sexual abuse survivor as the ultimate goal of therapy. It is an event that often occurs naturally as the client's sense of personal empowerment grows. Of course, there are many circumstances where the actual perpetrator is unknown or unavailable or where there would be unacceptable risks associated with a confrontation; the survivor can often accomplish a similar emotional outcome by imaginal confrontation. Writing letters that may never be mailed, visiting a grave, and use of role playing techniques may result in a sense of mastery and provide an emotional closure that eventually allows the survivor to forgive or let go.

If the survivor chooses to confront, careful preparation is strongly recommended. Although some attention should be given to the actual plans for carrying out the confrontation—place, time, what the survivor will say, and how he or she might reply to various responses—an exploration of the survivor's expectations should be the major therapeutic focus. Many survivors are hoping to achieve some specific reaction such as acknowledgement, validation, remorse, or even restitution. Although such hopes are understandable, they may set the survivor up for a devastating failure if they are emphasized as the goals of confrontation. The survivor is almost assured of success, however, if the stated goal is to break the silence surrounding the sexual abuse by telling the confronted person that it occurred.

When the survivor feels empowered in significant relationships and any posttraumatic symptoms have diminished to a tolerable level, the stage has been set for termination of therapy. The therapist must support the client's growth and potential autonomy by giving encouraging, accepting responses to client comments about "taking a vacation from therapy," "trying it on my own for a while," and so forth. Whenever possible, the survivor should be reassured that termination would not be absolute—that a return to therapy after a period of independence is possible. Attention to possible fears of abandonment, which may characterize survivors from extremely dysfunctional family backgrounds, may also become a major focus of this stage of therapy.

Conclusion

The complexity and difficulty of psychotherapy with adults molested as children is quite variable and depends on characteristics of the abuse experience and of the survivor's personality. When the abuse was especially severe, the family of origin was unsupportive, and early experiences in that family led to the creation of a personality disorder, treatment of the adult survivor can be long, arduous, and fraught with difficulties that threaten therapist burnout. The course of therapy may also be erratic because the survivor's lack of basic trust and oscillation between approach and avoidance of unresolved trauma.

Therapists must understand that the most severe treatment difficulties arise from a combination of personality disorder, unresolved trauma, and an overlay of revictimization experiences. The appropriate therapeutic stance is to be caring and consistent within firmly established therapeutic boundaries, to help the client who expresses readiness to explore the trauma and its effects, but to switch into a containment mode whenever indicated. This careful, titrated approach allows the client to go at his or her own pace. For some clients, this process will involve derepression and abreaction experiences. For all, the ultimate goal is to achieve a personal understanding of the effects of sexual abuse sufficient to allow a healthy realignment of significant relationships.

References

Bowlby, J. *A Secure Base: Parent-Child Attachment and Healthy Human Development.* New York: Basic Books, 1988.

Briere, J. *Therapy for Adults Molested as Children: Beyond Survival.* New York: Springer, 1989.

Briere, J. *Child Abuse Trauma: Theory and Treatment of the Lasting Effects.* Newbury Park, Calif.: Sage, 1992.

Courtois, C. A. *Healing the Incest Wound: Adult Survivors in Therapy.* New York: Norton, 1988.

Dolan, Y. M. *Resolving Sexual Abuse: Solution-Focused Therapy and Ericksonian Hypnosis for Adult Survivors.* New York: Norton, 1991.

Finkelhor, D. *Child Sexual Abuse: New Theory and Research.* New York: Free Press, 1984.

Gelinas, D. J. "The Persisting Negative Effects of Incest." *Psychiatry,* 1983, *46,* 312–332.

Gil, E. *Treatment of Adult Survivors of Childhood Abuse.* Walnut Creek, Calif.: Launch Press, 1988.

Herman, J. *Father-Daughter Incest.* Cambridge: Harvard University Press, 1981.

Herman, J., and Schatzow, E. "Recovery and Verification of Memories of Childhood Sexual Trauma." *Psychoanalytic Psychology,* 1987, *4,* 1–14.

Loftus, E. F. "The Reality of Repressed Memories." *American Psychologist,* 1993, *48,* 518–537.

Meiselman, K. C. *Resolving the Trauma of Incest: Reintegration Therapy with Survivors.* San Francisco: Jossey-Bass, 1990.

Russell, D.E.H. *The Secret Trauma: Incest in the Lives of Girls and Women.* New York: Basic Books, 1986.

KARIN C. MEISELMAN, *Ph.D., is a psychologist in private practice in Pasadena, California.*

Name Index

SUBJECT INDEX

ORDERING INFORMATION

NEW DIRECTIONS FOR MENTAL HEALTH SERVICES is a series of paperback books that presents timely and readable volumes on subjects of concern to clinicians, administrators, and others involved in the care of the mentally disabled. Each volume is devoted to one topic and includes a broad range of authoritative articles written by noted specialists in the field. Books in the series are published quarterly in Spring, Summer, Fall, and Winter and are available for purchase by subscription as well as individually.

SUBSCRIPTIONS for 1994 cost $54.00 for individuals (a savings of 25 percent over single-copy prices) and $75.00 for institutions, agencies, and libraries. Please do not send institutional checks for personal subscriptions. Standing orders are accepted.

SINGLE COPIES cost $17.95 when payment accompanies order. (California, New Jersey, New York, and Washington, D.C., residents please include appropriate sales tax.) All orders will be charged postage and handling.

DISCOUNTS FOR QUANTITY ORDERS are available. Please write to the address below for information.

ALL ORDERS must include either the name of an individual or an official purchase order number. Please submit your order as follows:
    Subscriptions: specify series and year subscription is to begin
    Single copies: include individual title code (such as MHS59)

MAIL ALL ORDERS TO:
    Jossey-Bass Publishers
    350 Sansome Street
    San Francisco, California 94104-1342

FOR SUBSCRIPTION SALES OUTSIDE OF THE UNITED STATES, contact any international subscription agency or Jossey-Bass directly.

OTHER TITLES AVAILABLE IN THE
NEW DIRECTIONS FOR MENTAL HEALTH SERVICES SERIES
H. Richard Lamb, Editor-in-Chief